D0038489

Successful Research Projects

To my spectacular family:
Simon, Agatha, and Linda

Bernard C. Beins

Ithaca College

Successful Research Projects

A Step-by-Step Guide

Los Angeles | London | New Delhi
Singapore | Washington DC

Los Angeles | London | New Delhi
Singapore | Washington DC

FOR INFORMATION:

SAGE Publications, Inc.
2455 Teller Road
Thousand Oaks, California 91320
E-mail: order@sagepub.com

SAGE Publications Ltd.
1 Oliver's Yard
55 City Road
London, EC1Y 1SP
United Kingdom

SAGE Publications India Pvt. Ltd.
B 1/I 1 Mohan Cooperative Industrial Area
Mathura Road, New Delhi 110 044
India

SAGE Publications Asia-Pacific Pte. Ltd.
3 Church Street
#10-04 Samsung Hub
Singapore 049483

Acquisitions Editor: Reid Hester
Associate Editor: Eve Oettinger
Editorial Assistant: Sarita Sarak
Production Editor: Eric Garner
Copy Editor: Lana Todorovic-Arndt
Typesetter: Hurix Systems Pvt. Ltd.
Proofreader: A. J. Sobczak
Indexer: Wendy Allex
Cover Designer: Karine Hovsepian
Marketing Manager: Lisa Sheldon Brown
Permissions Editor: Karen Ehrmann

Printed in the United States of America.

Library of Congress Cataloging-in-Publication Data

Beins, Bernard.

Successful research projects : a step-by-step guide / Bernard C.

Beins, Ithaca College.

pages cm

Includes bibliographical references and index.

ISBN 978-1-4522-0393-5 (pbk. : alk. paper)

1. Psychology—Research—Methodology.
2. Research—Methodology. 3. Report writing.
I. Title.

BF76.5.B4395 2013

150.72—dc23

2012043930

This book is printed on acid-free paper.

MIX
Paper from
responsible sources
FSC® C014174

13 14 15 16 17 10 9 8 7 6 5 4 3 2 1

Contents

Preface ❖

Why do psychologists do research? There are many answers to this question, but in my opinion, the best answer is that we do research because it is fun. People can be puzzling; research is a good way to assemble the pieces of the puzzle to help us understand those around us. This book will help you answer successfully your question about the way people behave.

I am assuming that you have already learned about the basic aspects of research. The material in this volume puts flesh on the bones as you embark on a project that you design and control. That is, when you learn the basics of research, you become aware of the general issues that are important in a good research design. But it may not be clear how to implement a project successfully. That is what this book is all about.

Throughout the book, I have made use of the research ideas that my students and I have developed to give you a sense of what kinds of questions you might ask, what research has already been done, what hypotheses you might pose, and how to develop your ideas. Over the past few decades, students have increasingly participated in conducting professional-quality research.

If you have the basic knowledge of research methodology, you can develop a research idea that will advance our psychological knowledge. It may not be apparent to you right now, but when you develop a successful research project, you are actually creating knowledge. That is, at the end of your research, you will know something that nobody else in the world knows. It will be new knowledge. This is always an exciting prospect.

As you can see by looking through the book, this volume will take you through each step of your project. First you have to develop a research idea. Other researchers have addressed many obvious and easy questions, and you probably don't want simply to repeat what others have done, so you need to figure out something else. You can make use of previous research to help you develop and refine your questions. I have described how you can generate new questions from what we already know.

In addition, I have given some important information about the ethics of research. If you are going to collect data using human or nonhuman animals, a review board must approve your work, so I have identified the practical issues regarding ethics that are associated with carrying out a project.

Before you begin the actual data collection, you need to identify your variables and methods of measurement. There is no single right way to address a question; you have options from which to choose. But I show how others have successfully done this so that you can too.

After you have collected your data, you will undoubtedly want to conduct statistical analyses. I have offered some basic information about dealing with your results and, after that, to make sense with interpretation and speculation about what the data tell you. In Appendix B, I have given some background on using IBM SPSS Statistics* to analyze the data with commonly used statistics.

Finally, you can see how to create a research report that is consistent with the guidelines set forth in the *Publication Manual of the American Psychological Association* (known as APA style). There are many useful resources for writing your report; I have not duplicated those books. Instead, I have outlined what you want to include in the various sections of your paper and how to develop your ideas in the various sections of the book.

Throughout your research, you have to pay attention to a lot of details, as I noted before. But if you are studying a topic that interests you, the process of generating a question and finding a way to answer it can be highly satisfying. No research project answers all the questions about a topic, but your research can be an important and interesting piece of the puzzle of human behavior.

Writing this book was like a research project: It involved collaboration among many people. I am grateful to Chris Cardone for her initial work in developing the idea for the book. In addition, Reid Hester and Sarita Sarak at SAGE were very helpful in guiding me through the final stages of the project. I also want to thank my copy editor, Lana Arndt, whose fastidious attention to detail helped generate the final form of this book.

Finally, my thanks to the reviewers who took time out from busy schedules to provide valuable feedback and insights:

Elizabeth Dretsch, Troy University

Shannon Hankhouse, Tarleton State University

Robert Michels, Santa Clara University

Vanessa Woodward, University of Southern Mississippi

---

*IBM SPSS Statistics was formerly called PASW® Statistics.

Chapter 1

Developing Your Research Idea

In this chapter you will learn about...

- ◆ Developing Your Ideas
- ◆ Refining Your Research Question
- ◆ Generating Your Hypothesis
- ◆ Figuring Out What Support for Your Hypothesis Would Look Like
- ◆ Preparing for Your Written Paper

When you conduct research, you create new knowledge. It is exciting to think that when you complete your project, you will know something that nobody else in the world knows. Your contribution to psychology may be quite modest; most research projects by professionals make small, incremental additions to our knowledge. But it can be a real contribution nonetheless.

The first step in the process involves developing a research idea. It is a little paradoxical, but coming up with a research idea is both easy and difficult. That is, there is a wealth of potential research questions that you might ask, so finding an interesting topic can be fairly easy, but figuring out exactly how you will approach the research question can be difficult. If an idea has occurred to you, there is a good chance that it has already occurred to somebody else. On the other hand, if others have studied a topic that interests you, you can use their ideas as a starting point for developing yours.

In this chapter, I will present some examples of how you could develop interesting and productive research projects. The examples are intended to reflect the process of developing ideas and certainly do not exhaust the range of possibilities.

I hope you will learn about strategies that lead to successful outcomes. Learning how to generate fruitful ideas may be the most important aspect of research.

The process involves quite a few separate steps and a lot of small decisions, but it all starts with your identification of a question that interests you and that other psychologists see as psychologically worthwhile.

Research is a multistep process. The ideas in this chapter relate to other aspects of the research process that you need to consider. But the identification of a research topic is a good place to start. Keep in mind that the later material, like use of PsycINFO to find work relevant to your ideas, will relate to what you are reading here. What you decide now will affect what happens later; at the same time, what you discover later may require that you revisit this chapter.

Developing Your Ideas

The first question to ask yourself as you embark on the quest for a research project is "What am I interested in?" If you want to research a topic, you will find it much more enjoyable if the topic interests you. The idea will really become yours. It is always possible that you will be fascinated by an idea that somebody else proposes, so don't discount that. But if you take on a task because of your interest in it, you are starting off on the right foot.

An immediate, but maybe not so obvious, source of ideas is you. Is there something about yourself that makes you wonder? For example, if you are left-handed, you have experiences that are different than those of right-handers in some instances. For example, can openers are constructed so that right-handers can use them most easily. Given that about 90% of people are right-handed, manufacturers are going to produce implements that favor right-handed people, which means that left-handed people will have to adapt. This need to adapt is not always benign. Coren and Halpern (1991) found that left-handers are at greater risk of accidents related to multiple aspects of life, as shown in Figure 1.1. Coren and Halpern also analyzed a set of existing data and discovered that mortality among left-handed people was notably greater than for right-handed people. Accidental deaths seem to play a large part in the death rates of left-handers, who have to adapt to a right-handed world. (After they published their findings, Coren and Halpern received a lot of criticism and even threats by people who thought that the authors were discriminating against left-handed people.)

One question that might arise from this kind of information is whether right-handed people would respond more negatively than left-handed people to opposite-handed implements. Left-handers are used to adapting, but right-handers are not. Or consider classroom desks with tablets made for right-handed people to take notes. Would a left-handed person enjoy a lecture if he or she had to take notes at a right-handed desk? Would it be any different

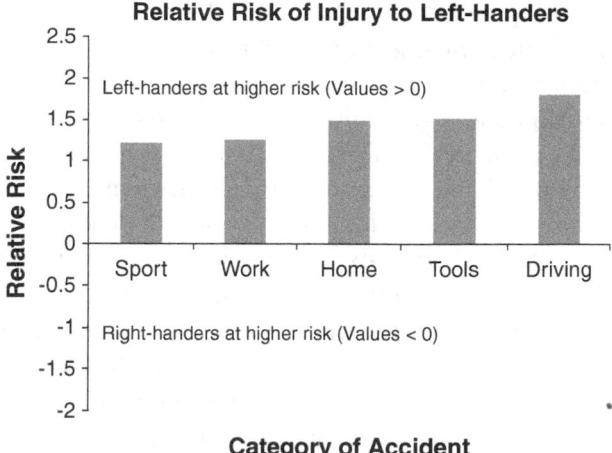

Figure 1.1   Relative risk of injury to left-handers by type of accident. Values greater than zero reflect greater risk for left-handers.

Source: Coren and Halpern (1991). Copyright © 1991 American Psychological Association. Reprinted with permission.

for a right-handed person at a left-handed desk? This kind of research project might provide useful information about helping people enjoy classes more.

Another fact about differences between left- and right-handers is that the two groups seem to respond to space around them differently. Casasanto (2009) found that his research participants had more positive associations to spaces on their dominant side in a two-choice situation. That is, right-handers preferred a given stimulus when it was on their right rather than on their left, and left-handers preferred it the other way around. It would be interesting to see if the liking was on a continuum such that the farther to the dominant side an object appeared, the more positively a person would rate it.

Considering that Coren and Halpern (1991) reported that left-handers are more likely to have accidents related to multiple aspects of life, you might focus on individual sports. Injuries in some sports may be more common among left-handers, but nobody has investigated that. Is it likely that some left-handers are more at risk in some sports? It is a question that has yet to be answered in the psychological literature.

A person's handedness is a seemingly small factor in one's life, but it could generate a host of interesting research projects. The same might be true of many different personal characteristics. For instance, would people who are overweight judge silhouettes of others differently depending on whether the silhouette depicted an overweight person? Do people with red hair rate others with red hair more positively than people with dark hair?

Thus, an initial question (e.g., Do left-handers and right-handers prefer stimuli on their dominant side?) can lead to new questions: Do redheads prefer redheads? One point to remember, though, is that it is possible to develop research questions that other psychologists would regard as unimportant or even trivial. So if you were going to see if red-haired people saw other red-haired people more positively than other hair colors, you would need to make a case about why this is an interesting psychological question.[1]

Casasanto's (2009) research about the relation between handedness and space preference was tied into the issue of the body specificity hypothesis. This hypothesis postulates that a person's interaction with the environment shapes the way the person thinks. The question of preference for hair color could be tied to the body specificity hypothesis, but it could also connect to something like the mere exposure effect, in which people develop a favorable reaction to something merely because of repeated exposure to it. In most cases, successful research questions connect to other psychological research.

As you will see in the next chapter, there are ways to find research that relates to a topic of interest to you. You will be able to see whether psychologists have paid attention to it. One of the most common ways to find out about existing research is through the database PsycINFO. As of 2011, there were more than 1,600 entries in PsycINFO in which the word *handedness* appeared in the title of the work. Some of them might not be of use to you. For instance, 99 of the works with *handedness* in the title involved nonhuman animals. These could be irrelevant to your project. Nonetheless, the fact that so many citations involve handedness indicates that the topic is of interest to psychologists.

In contrast, you might have to work a little harder in convincing others that a study of redheads is of psychological importance. As of 2011, there were five titles in PsycINFO that used *redhead*. One involved a study of finches, and another involved ducks, which is not exactly what we had in mind here. There were two studies of perceptions of hair color, and one that discovered that in 1947 (Von Hentig, 1947), there were more red-headed male criminals than you would predict based on the incidence of redheads in the general population. So the question of how people with red hair perceive the world around them is not, in and of itself, of particular interest to researchers. But if you tied your question to the issue of the mere

---

[1] A nonpsychological example of research that might make you wonder about its importance or interest involves the fact that somebody has discovered that William Shakespeare used 138,198 commas in his collective work (Bryson, 2007). Scholars have produced much interesting and important literary research about Shakespeare and his writing, but it seems hard to figure out how the number of commas fits into the overall body of work on him. Maybe it is of interest for reasons that psychologists would not appreciate.

exposure effect (121 citations in which *mere exposure effect* occurred in the PsycINFO abstract) or person perception (almost 1,500 citations), your idea would be more likely to resonate with other psychologists.

So you might reason that people with red hair are familiar with redheads because they see one every time they look into a mirror. This phenomenon might lead them to feel more positively about redheads than other people do. Or it might be that they favor redheads because such people are similar to them. Or they might not have any different impressions of redheads than they do of any other hair color. You would not know until you investigated.

You can also think about your own behavior (as opposed to your attitudes) in some important aspect of your life. For example, what factors affect your performance on tests in classes? Obviously, there are many to choose from. But one potentially interesting variable is how much sleep you get. Meijer and van den Wittenboer (2004) investigated sleep (and other variables) to see how they correlated with test performance. Surprisingly, the amount of research on the relation between sleep and learning in college students appearing in the literature is fairly small. Investigators have asked some of the obvious questions, but there are many yet to be addressed.

So far, I have identified strategies that will help you develop your research idea. But you should also pay attention to issues that need careful consideration as you develop your ideas. Every idea that you generate is not going to lead to a fruitful research project. Some projects may be trivial, whereas others may be too large or complex; some may be very difficult to complete successfully. Table 1.1 presents some of these issues.

Refining Your Research Question

Once you have an overall topic, you can specify the behaviors or attitudes that you want to measure and the variables that you think are related to or that cause some behavior to occur. After identifying your research topic, one of the next questions involves how you will set up your research.

Investigators adopt different approaches to their research. Those who work in laboratories often use experiments in which they manipulate variables in a controlled setting. Researchers who study people in everyday situations or ask for self-reports about behaviors and attitudes may use descriptive or survey research. Sometimes these categories overlap, but the difference between experimental and nonexperimental research is that experimental approaches permit you to make statements of causation: When condition A occurs, something happens because of it. When condition A does not occur, something else happens. It is the presence or absence of A that determines whether a behavior will occur.

Table 1.1   Potential Pitfalls to Consider When Generating a Research Project

The Issue	Comment
Too big a question	Just about every research project involves a small step beyond previous research, so keep your research question manageably small. Too large a question may require too many participants and too much time on your part. In addition, with very complex research, it can be quite difficult to interpret your results because there can be multiple variables interacting with one another.
The "so what" question	Some questions are fairly unimportant. For example, the effect of room color on studying for tests is one that most psychologists would probably consider unimportant. For something like this, you would have to make a case that it relates to recognizable psychological issues (Smith, 2007).
Lengthy projects	If you are conducting research as part of a class, your time may be limited to the duration of the academic term. It seems that research never proceeds as quickly as you think it is going to, so it is wise to create a methodology that is as compact as possible while still addressing your research question.
Projects requiring participants to return to a lab or to provide data on multiple occasions	Repeated measures designs allow you to collect a lot of data from a single person. But your participants' motivation is not likely to be as high as yours. So if your methodology requires people to work too hard (from their perspective), they may drop out.
Boundaries of competence	If you were to study personality using a projective test like the Rorschach Inkblot Test, there could be problems relating to your competence in scoring participants' answers. Some commercial tests are restricted so that only qualified people can acquire them, but the Rorschach stimuli are available on the Internet, so anybody could use them. If you were not qualified to use whatever tools or methodology is required for your research, you would be acting unethically.
Ethics in carrying out the study	If you develop a project that requires people or animals to be exposed to an experimental manipulation, you need to receive approval from your Institutional Review Board (or an Institutional Animal Care and Use Committee) or from somebody who is authorized to act on their behalf. You need authorization before you can even begin to recruit participants. This process can take a long time, so you should begin it as soon as possible.

The disadvantage of an experimental approach is that it generally involves a simplified laboratory experience that looks at only one or two variables at a time. We all know that our behaviors are usually the result of many variables. So experiments, particularly those that take place in a laboratory, may not tell us a lot about the way life operates on a daily basis.[2] Recent evaluation has indicated that social psychological research does generalize to life outside the lab to a certain degree, but there are some significant discrepancies between lab and field research; such discrepancies are less likely in industrial/organizational research (Mitchell, 2012).

In contrast, nonexperimental research that does not lead to cause-and-effect conclusions is still important because it also provides very useful and interesting information. Descriptive or correlational studies let us learn about relationships among variables. This approach often involves studying life as it normally unfolds. Thus, we can get a realistic idea of patterns of behavior involving multiple variables. The disadvantage of such research is that you don't know which of the many variables you know about (or might not be aware of) are affecting the behavior. You might be able to make predictions about behavior, but you don't know why it occurs that way.

One example might be the link between exposure to violent media and a person's level of aggression. Research has shown that people who are exposed to more violence are more violent in their behaviors. The relation is stronger than that between using (or not using) condoms and the incidence of HIV, which can lead to AIDS, and stronger than the association between exposure to lead and intelligence level in children, findings that are not at all controversial (Bushman & Anderson, 2001).

Nonetheless, many studies about media violence and violent behavior are correlational. Based on correlational approaches, we cannot determine whether exposure to violence causes violent behavior, whether violent behavior induces people to seek out violent media, or whether some other factors are causing both. In fact, some psychologists have made the argument that we still do not know if there is a causal link (e.g., Ferguson, 2002), although Anderson and Bushman (2002) pointed out that there have been over 150 experiments (which can lead to causal conclusions) showing a connection between aggression and exposure to media violence.

---

[2]You shouldn't assume that laboratory studies have no validity regarding everyday life. One extreme example involves Stanley Milgram's obedience studies. His original work was laboratory based and involved him asking the research participants to engage in behaviors that they would never do in the course of normal life. But his conclusions turn out to have wide generalizability outside the laboratory.

So what does this mean for your research? It means that you could choose to do an experiment, most likely in a laboratory, that investigated one or two variables to see if they have an effect on behavior, thought, or attitude. The context would be a simplified version of everyday behavior with many important variables stripped away. You would have control over what happens, so your conclusions might be clear and straightforward about cause and effect. But it would be a simplified version of life.

On the other hand, if you did a correlational study, you could study behaviors not possible in an experiment. If you wanted to know if somebody who was frustrated was likely to engage in violence against another person, it would be unethical to set up that kind of situation. But you could do a correlational survey study to see whether frustration leads to aggression. There might be an association. The drawback is that you wouldn't necessarily know if it was the frustration that led to the violence.

You might also consider an observational study. Such an approach could provide information about actual violence rather than simply a self-report, which may or may not be accurately remembered or reported. An observational study would involve realistic situations and actual behavior. Unfortunately, you might have to wait a long time to observe the behavior of interest.

No matter what methodology you use, it will have its own strengths and its own weaknesses. You should be aware of them so you can make a choice that is sensible given your circumstances.

Generating Your Hypothesis

Sometimes research projects begin with the question "I wonder what would happen if . . ." This kind of question can lead to interesting research, but there is a good chance that if your question is one that would be of interest to psychologists, somebody has already conducted research on the topic.

So rather than simply repeating an earlier question, you might want to take a previous idea and see what new ideas it can generate. Replicating an earlier study in a very similar way might be a good idea if there is reason to believe that the original research had gaps that you could fill, but most psychologists want to go beyond previous ideas.

You can find out what other investigators have done pretty easily. That is the topic of the next chapter, but at this point, I will describe how you go about generating a hypothesis so that your research question is more like "I'll bet that this is what will happen, and this is why . . ." The earlier research will help you develop expectations, that is, hypotheses, that you can test.

Consider, for example, that people respond to stimuli without being consciously aware that they are doing so. For instance, Bargh, Chen, and Burrows (1996) primed participants with stereotypes of old age. The participants rearranged words to form sentences in which the words were associated with the elderly, like *bingo, forgetful, retired, wrinkle, rigid,* and *traditional*. In a control condition, neutral words like *thirsty* and *clean* replaced the age-related words (p. 236).

In two experiments, the original study and a replication study, as the participants left the lab, a confederate in the hallway surreptitiously timed how long it took the participant to walk the length of the hall. People who were primed with age-related words actually walked more slowly than those primed with neutral words, as shown in Figure 1.2.

The study by Bargh et al. (1996) related to automatic behavior, that is, behavior that people engage in without being consciously aware of it. But you could extend the study to find out if people show a reverse phenomenon. That is, would people walk faster if they had been primed to think of energetic, young children who never seem to move slowly? This type of finding might have notable implications for the elderly, but you could set up a study in which college-aged participants (such as those Bargh et al. relied on) were primed with thoughts of youthful energy.

Your hypothesis might be that people who are exposed to stereotypes of a different group will walk at speeds resembling the group about whom they are primed. A further question is whether being primed regarding

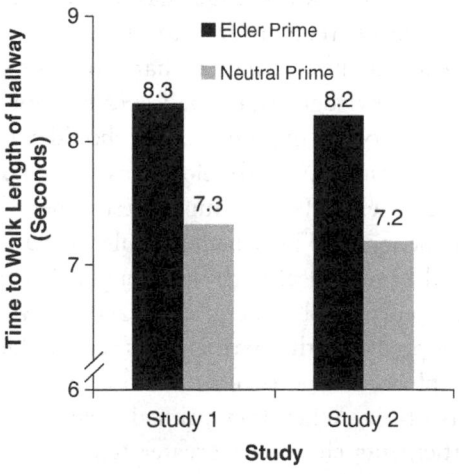

Figure 1.2   Time taken to walk the length of a hallway after being primed with words associated with old age or with words unrelated to age.

Source: Bargh, J. A., et al. Copyright © 1996 American Psychological Association. Reprinted with permission.

people of a participant's own age group in a certain way, like watching a video of a person either running or walking with a cane or a crutch, would make a difference in the participant's walking speed.

Based on the research of others, you can generate your own question with your own prediction of what will happen. If you know what has already happened, it will help you predict what will happen when you change things a little bit. As always, the more you know to begin with, the easier it will be to design your study and to generate hypotheses that your data will eventually support.

Figuring Out What Support for Your Hypothesis Would Look Like

When you plan your study, you can use theory and the results of previous research to form expectations about your results. That is, you set up hypotheses to see if people behave the way you expect them to. In many cases, the outcomes of research are in full agreement with the hypotheses, but sometimes the results do not conform to expectations.

Professional researchers probably receive support for their hypotheses a high percentage of the time because they often have substantial knowledge of the topic they are studying and are moving one small step forward in each project. Consequently, each small step follows nicely from the previous one.

On the other hand, if you are conducting a study in an area about which you are not highly familiar, your hypotheses may not lead to the results you expect. That is, your level of knowledge may not be sufficient to predict accurately how the variables relate to one another. Or if you are investigating an area that is relatively new, it may be hard to make sound predictions because fundamental knowledge about the issues has not yet emerged.

In any case, when you form a hypothesis, you should come up with predictions that are as specific and as well developed as possible. And they should relate to your measurements. For example, researchers have investigated terror management theory (TMT), which postulates that people are aware of their mortality and have to deal with the thought that they will die some day. Based on the theory, Goldenberg, Pyszczynski, McCoy, Greenberg, and Solomon (1999) predicted that participants scoring high in neuroticism would associate the physical aspects of sex with death but would not do so for romantic aspects of sex. When they primed participants on the physical dimension, the participants showed a greater tendency to complete word fragments (e.g., *S K _ _ L*, which could be completed either as *skull* or *skill*) with death-related themes than participants in the romantic prime condition.

So my students and I wondered whether jokes about sex would have the same effect as the primes of Goldenberg et al. (1999). We assessed neuroticism level using a brief 10-item inventory from the Oregon Research

Institute (ipip.ori.org) and established groups of low-, medium-, and high-neuroticism participants. After participants read and rated the funniness of sex-themed jokes, they completed word fragments, some of which could lead to death-related words.

With respect to our hypotheses, we reasoned that if TMT's predictions held true for Goldenberg's participants, then the theory might hold true for jokes as well: Our participants might generate a greater number of death-related words when completing the word fragments. Specifically, we hypothesized that as participant levels increased, the number of death-related word fragments that they generated would also increase.

Our hypothesis was partially confirmed. That is, high-neuroticism participants generated more death-related words than did either of the other groups; the other two groups did not differ significantly. The results appear in Figure 1.3. The predictions of TMT held true, revealing that, instead of leading to socially positive responses, some humor may actually result in negative outcomes for high-neuroticism people.

In this example, we created groups based on participants' levels of neuroticism and made a prediction about their behavior related to our dependent variable, the number of word fragments they completed that

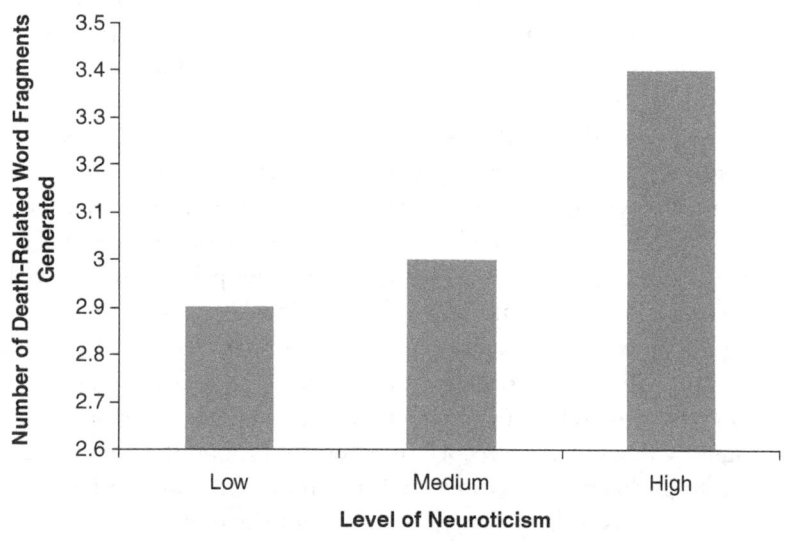

Figure 1.3   Number of Death-Related Words Generated by Participants with Varying Levels of Neuroticism.

Source: Dietz, A. P., Albowicz, C., & Beins, B. C. (2011, October). *Neuroticism and sex-related jokes: Predictions from terror management theory.* Poster presentation at the annual convention of the New England Psychological Association, Fairfield, CT. Copyright Bernard C. Beins. Used with permission.

had death-related themes. In advance, we knew what our results would look like with respect to the independent and dependent variables if those results supported our hypotheses. Fortunately, the results were in accord with our hypothesis.

Preparing for Your Written Paper

When you complete your project, it is likely that you will write a report of your research. Here is some guidance that will help you organize the introduction section of your paper.

Authors typically include several different elements in the introduction. One of these elements is an overview of the research question. You can begin your introduction with a statement about the topic that engages the reader's interest. In this section, you prepare your reader for your research by providing some background information on how your ideas developed. Another feature of the introduction is a review of research that investigators have published or presented. This review does not need to be exhaustive, but it should give the reader a sense of what researchers know about the topic and provide a description of the theory and research related to the topic.

The final part of the introduction is a presentation of your hypothesis. That is, based on what others have already done, what do you expect to occur in your research? You should provide the logic that leads from the earlier research to yours.

It will be a good idea to address the questions listed in Table 1.2 as you read the material. If you write a brief statement in which you answer each question in the table, you will gain two benefits. First, you will be recording the ideas while they are fresh in your mind. Second, you will have a record of the source of the ideas; it can be quite frustrating if, at some later point, you need to document the source of an idea and cannot remember where you found it.

Using the table below may seem like a lot of work, but it will pay off in the end. You will form a good sense of the research that others have done, you won't have to rely on your memory about what other investigators have found, you will have a record of where you found the material in case you need to go back and get more information, and you will have a well-formed set of ideas to help you write your introduction.

Finally, when you write your paper, quite possibly you will use APA style. The basics of APA style appear in Appendix A.

Table 1.2   Information to Record as You Read Background Information for Your Research

Reference Citation in APA Style

Question	Important Points
What research question did the investigators ask?	• What was the main source (or sources) of their ideas? • What did they hypothesize that relates to your work? • Why did they develop the hypothesis? They may have addressed several questions, but you should focus on the questions that relate to your ideas.
What was their methodology?	• Who were their participants or subjects? • What apparatus or materials did they use? • What procedure did they use in the research? That is, what did their participants or subjects actually do? • What were their independent and dependent variables? That is, what were their operational definitions and what did they actually measure?
What did they find?	• Was their hypothesis supported? • What were the important descriptive statistics (e.g., means)? • What were the important inferential statistics (e.g., F values, r values)?
What did they conclude?	• How did they interpret their results? • What did they say was novel about their findings? That is, what do they know now that they didn't know before they did their study? • How do their results relate to your idea?

Chapter 2
Expanding Your Knowledge

In this chapter you will learn about...

- ◆ Sources of Ideas
- ◆ PsycINFO—Finding Research That Psychologists Have Already Carried Out

Sources of Ideas

Everyday Behaviors and Occurrences

One way you can begin to develop ideas for potential research projects is through attention to behavior in the world around you. Probably the most extensive, and maybe the most famous, line of research arising this way dealt with the issue of bystander intervention and diffusion of responsibility. It involved a tragic incident in the early 1960s in which a woman named Kitty Genovese was murdered in New York City. The *New York Times* printed a detailed story of the murder and, as it turns out, got most of the important details wrong (Manning, Levine, & Collins, 2007). For example, the *Times* article said that there were 38 people who watched a man stalk and kill Kitty Genovese, when it would have literally been impossible for more than two or three people to have actually seen the murder.

In any case, two psychologists, John Darley and Bibb Latané, read the article and asked why the supposed witnesses didn't help the victim. This led to a classic study on helping behavior (Darley & Latané, 1968) and a long string of related research over the decades. Fortunately, you are not likely to encounter such a brutal incident, but you may see people behave in a certain way in your own life and wonder why. If that happens, you have a potential research project on your hands.

In another area, people have noted that aggression increases when the temperature is high. This observation has led to considerable research. For instance, investigators wondered whether it affects aggression in sporting events. Reifman, Larrick, and Fein (1991) and, later, Larrick, Timmerman, Carton, and Abrevaya (2011) reported that pitchers in baseball are more likely to hit a batter on the other team in hot weather and to retaliate when a player on their team is hit by a pitched ball thrown by the opposing pitcher when the weather is hot but less likely to retaliate when it is cold.

You might ask if there is a similar pattern in other sports, such as football, for which extensive records exist. Or it might be the case that people have less patience in general during hot weather. Are drivers more likely to be impatient and less likely to come to a full stop at a stop sign when it is hot? Or are people waiting in a line more likely to be rude in hot weather when waiting in line to get a cold drink? These are simple questions, but they may be worth asking in a research project.

As I noted above, if research questions like these strike you as interesting, you should find out what other researchers think about them. In many cases, questions that are obvious to you are also obvious to others, who may have already answered them. In that case, you probably would not proceed to repeat their research exactly as they did it. But even if other psychologists have answered your question, you may be able to take what they did and expand on it. For example, returning to consideration of left-handedness, consider that Coren and Halpern (1991) found that left-handers suffer injuries requiring medical attention more than right-handers. But they did not assess the differences, if any, in minor injuries from everyday activity. Furthermore, those researchers included sporting injuries in their analysis, but they did not break down those injuries by sport. They provided some basic information, but it would be possible for you to go beyond what they discovered.

Previous Research

It is not an exaggeration to say that the more you know about psychological topics and issues, the better your research ideas will be. Part of this effect is due to the fact that when you know a lot, you can tie various threads together in ways that others have not yet done. For example, my students and I have studied humor appreciation in our research (Beins & O'Toole, 2010; Wimer & Beins, 2008). Some of the research has dealt with personality, specifically the five-factor theory, and we have studied the link between neuroticism scores and joke ratings.

Previous research had revealed that people who score high on neuroticism tend not to like nonsense jokes as well as people scoring low on that trait

(Galloway & Chirico, 2008). This finding led us to think about other types of jokes that high scorers may evaluate differently from low scorers.

A different line of research, on terror management theory (TMT), showed that people scoring high in neuroticism generated thoughts of death when primed with physical aspects of sex compared to romantic aspects of sex, whereas that pattern did not emerge among people scoring low in neuroticism (Goldenberg, Pyszczynski, McCoy, Greenberg, & Solomon, 1999).

So as you read in Chapter 1, my research team, using jokes as stimuli, investigated the prediction of TMT that people scoring high on neuroticism would think of death when primed with physical aspects of sex. We presented a series of sex-themed jokes to research participants, measured their level of neuroticism, and asked them to complete word fragments that could lead either to death-related words or to neutral words (e.g., *COFF_ _* could be completed either as *coffin* or *coffee*).

The result was that those high in neuroticism completed significantly more word fragments with death-related words than did those low in neuroticism. These results gave support to TMT.

This research project arose from two quite different areas of psychology. One involved humor appreciation and the other involved concerns about death. The two areas coalesced nicely and led to an interesting and fruitful research project. If we were not knowledgeable across these different domains of psychology, we would not have developed the ideas that we did. There were over 400 PsycINFO citations for *terror management theory* and over 6,000 for *humor*, but there was none that combined the two.

Finding Sources That Present Possible Research Ideas

As I noted above, you can be your own source of interesting research questions. There are undoubtedly behaviors of your own that you could investigate. They can include topics that are so normal that you overlook them. But there are also external sources where you can find research topics.

One obvious source is a research journal. There are more journals that publish psychological research than you might think. For instance, there are over 150 journals that publish research related to cross-cultural psychology; they may not all be devoted strictly to this area, but they do have articles on the topic. There are over 50 on the interaction between psychology and the law. (There is a convenient online list at journalseek.net/psyc.htm.)

If you have access to these journals in your library, you can look at their tables of contents to see what topics other psychologists have studied. In many cases, even if your library does not carry the journals, you can access their tables of contents online. Often, your library will allow access to journals through various databases it has available.

There are also online sites that describe lines of research that you might be interested in pursuing. Professor John Krantz of the Psychology Department at Hanover College maintains a website that lists studies in which you can participate and provide data (psych.hanover.edu/research/exponnet.html). These studies can give you a sense of what research is taking place in different areas of psychology, and you can develop research along the same lines. Table 2.1 lists a few of the different areas of psychology listed on that website and provides examples of the titles of the projects.

Table 2.1   Examples of Research Studies Posted Online by Area Within Psychology

Area of Psychology	Examples of Research
Cognition	A study on how sleep affects memory and thinking skills Human navigation in virtual environments
Consumer Psychology	Choice of mobile phones Personality and entertainment preferences
Cyber Psychology	Deception and lying on the Internet Narcissism, vanity and gossip in a social networking environment
Developmental	Perceptions of children's behavior Parenting goals of fathers and mothers of teenagers
Emotions	Recognition of emotion through dance Good or bad? Rating the positivity or negativity of statements
Environmental Psychology	Jekyll v. Hyde: The social context of pro-environmental behaviour Goal setting and sustainability
Forensic Psychology	A quick survey regarding views of a defendant Criminal justice attitudes and jury decision making
Gender	The cultural intersection of gender role orientation and race as indicators of body dissatisfaction Men matters: Men's personalities and social lives
General	Opinions about science Positive life experiences
Health Psychology	Self and health behaviours Time perspective, gratitude and well-being
Industrial/Organizational	Hostile workplace climate Work related preferences and behaviour

Judgment and Decision	Would you drink that?
	Responding to moral dilemmas
Linguistics	Instruction giving in virtual environments
	Vague use of language
Mental Health	Anxiety, depression and the risks of everyday life
	Personal values and well-being
Personality Psychology and Religion	Religion and moral dilemmas
Relationships	Would you date me?
	Romantic relationships and solitude
Sensation and Perception	Is there a cross-cultural perception of portrayed emotions in music?
Sexuality	Beliefs about sex and relationships
	Male judgments of female facial attractiveness
Social Cognition	Face impressions
	Online shopping study
Social Psychology	What are you laughing at?
	Self-perception in social groups

Source: http://psych.hanover.edu/research/exponnet.html.

As you can see, there is a wealth of topics. The titles can give you clues to the issues that psychologists are investigating. If you participate in some of the studies, you will see the methodologies that they are using. Further, you can search in the research literature for journal articles that the psychologists conducting the online studies have written.

There are also websites that present science news that includes psychological and other behavioral research. For instance, the website Science Daily (www.sciencedaily.com) reports on the latest science news in areas titled "Health & Medicine" and "Mind and Brain." You could get useful topics for your research at this site.

One story reported on that website had the headline "Scientists Highlight Link Between Stress and Appetite." The first paragraph gave a quick overview.

Science Daily (Aug. 13, 2011)—Researchers in the Hotchkiss Brain Institute (HBI) at the University of Calgary's Faculty of Medicine have uncovered a mechanism by which stress increases food drive in rats. This new discovery, published online this week in the journal *Neuron*, could provide important insight into why stress is thought to be one of the underlying contributors to obesity (Scientists Highlight Link, 2011).

As you can see, the researchers used an animal model to test their hypothesis, but there is no reason that you could not adapt the ideas for human populations. For example, when tests are imminent, student stress levels may increase. If that happens, their eating habits may change before tests. Other research has shown a link between sleep deprivation and obesity. It might be instructive to see if students who do not sleep normally or sufficiently prior to tests also eat less well than normal.

There are other sources as well. The *Monitor on Psychology* published monthly by the American Psychological Association offers brief summaries of interesting research. So does the *Observer*, a publication of the Association for Psychological Science, which presents brief excerpts from the popular press. One such summary originally appeared in the *Los Angeles Times*. The researchers discovered that when they presented a set of instructions on how to make sushi, participants concluded that the recipe was more difficult when they read the instructions in a hard-to-read font than when the instructions were in an easier font (On the Newsstand, 2009). Thus, the participants confused the form of the message with the content of the message. Based on the information in a news story, you can often locate the original research; in this case, the news report was based on research by two psychologists, Hyunjin Song and Norbert Schwarz (Song & Schwarz, 2008).

You might take this research as a starting point and investigate whether this effect holds true for easy tasks and for hard tasks, for familiar tasks and for unfamiliar tasks, or for classroom learning. Subsequent to this research, Song and Schwarz published a related article that documented the fact that people associate hard-to-pronounce words with risk (Song & Schwarz, 2009). This finding might relate to the mere exposure effect, so you might hypothesize that exposing people to a hard-to-pronounce word might reduce their discomfort with it. You could use the methodology of Song and Schwarz to develop your own approach.

PsycINFO—Finding Research That Psychologists Have Already Carried Out

After you have decided on an idea for your project, you can start a systematic search for research related to it. One of the most convenient and comprehensive sources of information about the research that investigators have already published is through the database PsycINFO. This database contains descriptions of just about any research published in a psychological journal; it also provides information about books in psychology.

There are different electronic platforms associated with PsycINFO, but the search process is fairly similar in each. The elements that you are most likely to use in starting your PsycINFO search are the subject (i.e., the topic), the descriptors and keywords, and the author, although there are other fields that can be helpful.

Suppose you want to find a study on dating among college students. The easiest (but not the most advisable) approach would be to search for *dating* anywhere in the PsycINFO record. As of late in 2011, if you searched for *dating* without specifying anything other than the word, you would have gotten over 5,600 hits. Unfortunately, many of them would have related to aspects that might not interest you. For instance, one citation would be research on ambiguous romantic situations, a topic that might be interesting, but not what you were looking for (Epstude & Förster, 2011).

To narrow down the search, it helps to make use of the thesaurus in PsycINFO, a feature that indicates the specific term that PsycINFO uses in classifying research. For this example, the thesaurus would specify using the term *social dating*. In addition, to maximize the number of relevant hits, you can specify that *social dating* is the subject (or the descriptor) of your search. On the same day that a broad search for *dating* led to over 5,600 hits, limiting the search to social dating as the subject led to more than 2,600 hits, fewer than half the number in the original search. You can count on that work being related to the topic you want to pursue when you use the thesaurus. You still wouldn't want to read through 2,600 sources, so you could limit your search even further. If you limit the hits to studies published between January 2000 and January 2010 with young adults as participants, with research published in peer-reviewed journals in English, and with no dissertations, you would find just over 300 relevant records.

As you refine your search, you can narrow down the number of records you get until you have identified the relevant parameters of your search. At this point, you might have a small enough number of relevant articles that will not overwhelm you as you read the titles and descriptions to see if they match your interests.

Table 2.2 presents some ways to limit the number of hits you get to a manageable number. This reduction can save you time, but you need to be smart in your searches—you don't want to eliminate from your search a lot of sources that could be valuable to you. The example in Table 2.2 shows how you might conduct your search if you wanted to conduct a study related to study habits of college students. If you simply typed *studying* into PsycINFO and specified only that you wanted all the citations that had this word in the text of the citation, you would see that there are over 29,000 items that fell into that category, most of which would be irrelevant

Table 2.2   Ways to Reduce Irrelevant Hits in PsycINFO Searches (as of Late in 2011) Using the EBSCO Platform for Searching for Research About Student Study Habits[†]

Strategies in Advanced Searches to Reduce Hits[*]	Example Relating to Studying in School
Use the appropriate term from PsycINFO's thesaurus. You can start by typing in a word that relates to your topic of interest and see what it relates to in the thesaurus (e.g., *study habits* rather than *studying* or *social dating* rather than simply *dating*).	The thesaurus term is *study habits*. If you search in *All Text*, you get 3,252 records.
Search using *Subject* or *Descriptor* rather than searching for any use of a word	If you use *study habits* and narrow the search to *Subject* (*Descriptor*), you get 2,328 records.
Using the *Advanced Search* feature, limit the subject population.	If you limit your search to *young adults,* which means 18 to 29 years of age, you get 188 records.
Using the Advanced Search feature, limit the search to articles in *Peer-Reviewed Journals.*	If you limit the search to peer-reviewed journals, which are likely to present research conducted by professionals, you end up with 140 records.
Using the Advanced Search feature, limit the search to articles in the *Range of Years* from 2000 to 2010.	If you limit the search to this time period, you get 98 records. Sometimes you may want only recent research, but remember that you can find older research that will help you create your study.
Using the Advanced Search feature, limit the search to articles to which you have *Full-Text Access Electronically.***	If you limit the search to journal articles that you can get online (at least with the databases that I have available), you get 55 records.

[†]Features and terms may differ slightly across platforms.
[*]Note: Each successive step keeps the previous limitation in place in this example.
[**]Not all platforms may have this feature.

to you. The table shows how you could avoid this overwhelming number of hits. This is not the only strategy, but it will give you a sense of how to approach your own search.

Sometimes you may search for research and find very little that relates to your topic. In this case, you want to expand your search. One common way is to use so-called wild cards in your search. Psychologists have discussed the importance of sense of humor when two people are romantically attracted to one another. So if you wanted to study the link between humor and romantic involvement, you could search for *humor* as the subject and get around 4,000 hits, many of which would not be of interest to you.

If you then decided to narrow your search to *humor* as the subject and the word *romance* anywhere in the PsycINFO record, you would get fewer than 20 hits, which might be too few. At this point, you could use a wild card to broaden the search. Using an asterisk (*) tells PsycINFO to search for all words beginning with the letters prior to the asterisk. Searching for *humor* as the subject and *roman** anywhere in the text tells PsycINFO to search for records that have *humor* as the subject and any word beginning with the letters *roman* (e.g., *romantic, romance*). Doing that would lead to over 40 hits, over double the original number.

You could further expand the number of hits by telling PsycINFO to search for *roman** OR *dating*. To do this, you simply type *roman** OR *dating* as your search term. As of late 2011, this strategy led to additional hits that dealt either with humor and romance or humor and dating.

Table 2.3 identifies some other ways to find relevant material to help you in your search. None of these alone will guarantee that you will find every possible source, but they raise the probability that you will find the information you need to develop your research.

Table 2.3   Additional Approaches to Finding Information Relevant to Your Research

Approach	What This Approach Will Do
Find an author who has published on your topic and see what else he or she has done by searching by *Author* in PsycINFO.	If you can identify a key figure in the field, you can find what the person has published. Then you can find useful subject headings and keywords to enter into your search. You can also search to find who has cited this author.
Look in a journal with a relevant title.	If you are studying violence, for example, you can search for relevant articles in a journal like *Psychology of Violence*.
Find a classic article and see what other publications have used it as a reference. Some databases allow you to search specifically to see what publications cite a specific author or a specific title appears.	Using PsycINFO, you can search for articles that cite work that has been influential in the field. You can then see what other work cites each new publication you have found.

(continued)

Table 2.3   (continued)

Approach	What This Approach Will Do
Do an Internet search using the title of an article.	Sometimes authors post their published work on their own websites. If you find such work, you can often see what else the person has done in the area.
Ask a faculty member.	There may be people in your department who can direct you to relevant sources. If such people provide even a single reference citation, you can use that information to find others.

Chapter 3

Acting Ethically in Your Research

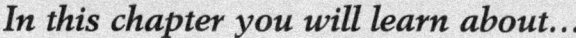

In this chapter you will learn about...

◆ Ethical Principles and Standards of the American Psychological Association

◆ Federal Regulations in the United States

◆ Important Ethical Issues in Psychological Research

◆ Preparing for Evaluation by Your Institutional Review Board

◆ Commonly Requested Information for IRB Proposals

Most people, researchers included, act responsibly and ethically most of the time. Nonetheless, there have been enough instances of questionable research in the past century that governments have found it necessary to establish formal guidelines and to pass laws regulating research.

Most of the famous instances of ethically troublesome research have not involved psychology. The two psychological cases frequently cited are Stanley Milgram's obedience studies (Milgram, 1974) and Philip Zimbardo's prison studies (Zimbardo, 1973). The American Psychological Association (APA) actually investigated Milgram regarding the ethics of his research when he applied to become a member. APA concluded that Milgram had not committed ethical breaches.

Both of these famous cases occurred about four decades ago. It is hard to believe that there have been no serious cases hidden within the psychological literature since then, but if you look in psychology journals, you will see that most research is fairly benign with respect to potential harm to participants or subjects.

Ethical Principles and Standards of the American Psychological Association

APA first developed ethical principles for its members over half a century ago (American Psychological Association, 1953). The ethics code has undergone periodic revision several times since then, with a revision in 2002 (American Psychological Association, 2002) and an update in 2010 (2010 Amendments, 2010). The Code of Conduct in its entirety is available online at www.apa.org/ethics/code/index.aspx.

Table 3.1   Summary of General Principles of the Code of Conduct Adopted by the American Psychological Association

Principle	What It Means
Principle A: Beneficence and Nonmaleficence	Strive to ensure that actions benefit people and do no harm.
Principle B: Fidelity and Responsibility	Psychologists establish relationships of trust with those with whom they work and accept appropriate responsibility for their behavior.
Principle C: Integrity	Psychologists seek to represent psychological science accurately and truthfully; they do not misrepresent facts or engage in intentionally invalid interpretations of research or assessment.
Principle D: Justice	Psychologists exercise reasonable judgment and strive to recognize their biases and the limitations to their competence so that they do no harm.
Principle E: Respect for People's Rights and Dignity	Psychologists respect people and recognize their human rights.

Source: American Psychological Association. (2002). Ethical principles of psychologists and code of conduct. *American Psychologist, 57,* 1060–1073. Used with permission.

General Principles

The ethics code consists of two general elements, a statement of principles designed to guide psychologists to aspire to the highest level of professional conduct and a set of standards that, if violated, can lead to sanctions by APA. Members of APA (including student members) are obligated to follow this Code of Conduct.

There are five general principles that APA has adopted as a set of ideas. A summary of the principles appears in Table 3.1.

Ethical Standards

The Code of Conduct adopted by APA also contains enforceable standards that its members are obligated to follow. The standards resemble legal regulations but are specific to psychology. The Code consists of 10 components, many of which relate to the work of professional psychologists engaged in therapy with clients.

Standard 8 deals with research and publication and is the standard most germane to your activity. As you can see in Table 3.2, there are 15 components to this standard. Because the standard is meant for professional researchers, there are elements that may not pertain to your project.

The standard is fairly clear and should be easy to follow. If you are contemplating research with people, the sections that will likely relate to your research include Sections 8.01, 8.02, 8.05, 8.07, 8.10, and 8.11. If you will be using nonhuman animals, you will need to seek approval from your Institutional Animal Use and Care Committee and follow the guidelines in Section 8.09. In rare cases, your work may involve the other sections, but for student projects, they probably will not matter.

Federal Regulations in the United States

The APA Code of Conduct is relevant to you because your research is psychological. But there are legal regulations that affect researchers from all disciplines. The federal regulations were instituted in the 1970s and have undergone periodic review. The regulations change at times, so it is always a good idea to refer to them or to seek guidance from a researcher who is familiar with them.

Table 3.2   Ethical Standards Established by the American Psychological
                 Association (APA) Regarding Research and Publication

Standard 8: Research and Publication

Standard	How It Is Likely to Affect You
8.01 Institutional Approval	You need to obtain approval from your school's Institutional Review Board (IRB) before starting recruitment of participants or data collection.
8.02 Informed Consent to Research	When collecting data, you need to inform participants about • Purpose, length, and procedures of your study • Their right to decline participation and to withdraw at any time • The consequences of withdrawing (There should be no penalties in nonclinical, psychological research.) • Potential risks or other negative aspects of participation (Most psychological research is relatively free of risks or negative aspects.) • Benefits from participating in the research • Limits of confidentiality (In most nonclinical research, there should be complete confidentiality.) • Incentives for participating (This is often extra credit in a class.) • A person to contact in case of questions or concerns NOTE: APA has guidelines for research involving clinical treatment. These are not likely to be relevant in your research.
8.03 Informed Consent for Recording Voices and Images in Research	You must receive prior permission from research subjects for recording their voices or images • Unless the research involves naturalistic observation *and* will not lead to personal identification or harm *or* • The research involves deception, in which case permission must be obtained during debriefing.
8.04 Client/Patient, Student, and Subordinate Research Participants	If participants have the opportunity for extra credit, you must make sure that they have nonresearch options for such credit. Otherwise, you cannot recruit them for extra credit.
8.05 Dispensing With Informed Consent for Research	This provision is not likely to apply to you, although if you are conducting online research, the method of documenting informed consent will not involve an actual paper document. You should consult your adviser or your IRB.

8.06 Offering Inducements for Research Participation	You are not allowed to offer excessive inducement that would make it hard for a person to turn you down.
8.07 Deception in Research	You should minimize the use of deception. • If it necessary for the conduct of your research, you need to debrief subjects as soon as possible, preferably at the end of the testing session. • You may not deceive participants regarding risk or other averse effects.
8.08 Debriefing	• You should explain to participants the purpose of the research and the outcome, correcting any potential misconceptions about the topic. • If harm has occurred, the researcher must take reasonable steps to minimize the effects.
8.09 Humane Care and Use of Animals in Research	• Researchers must care for animals according to federal, state, and local laws. Use of nonhuman animals requires oversight by a psychologist trained in care of and research with animals. • Supervising psychologists must train those working under their auspices. • Researchers should avoid inflicting pain or discomfort on animals; if it is necessary, it should be at the most minimal level for conduct of the study.
8.10 Reporting Research Results	• Psychologists should not fabricate data. • If a researcher discovers an error in the data, the error should be corrected.
8.11 Plagiarism	You must give credit to others for their work or their data.
8.12 Publication Credit	Psychologists should be listed as coauthors only for work to which they have contributed significantly.
8.13 Duplicate Publication of Data	If you have completed publishable work, it may appear in only one publication (unless it is in a book or other publication that clearly involves reprinted work).
8.14 Sharing Research Data for Verification	If another researcher requests your data, you must share the data with that person.
8.15 Reviewers	As a student, you are not likely to be a reviewer of a professional's work, but if you are, you must maintain confidentiality about that work.

Source: American Psychological Association. (2002). Ethical principles of psychologists and code of conduct. *American Psychologist, 57,*1060–1073. Adapted with permission.

Note: Some standards are typically not relevant to student research. This table gives an overview of how the APA standards would affect you and are abridged. A complete listing of the standards is available at www.apa.org/ethics/code/index.aspx.

Because the vast majority of notable cases with ethical problems have involved medical or biological research with people, the federal guidelines in the United States were written with prevention of problems in those domains in mind. For example, there were instances of researchers who administered food with radioactive substances to institutionalized children without any informed consent (ACHRE, n.d.), full-body irradiation of terminal cancer patients without permission (Rothman, 1994), and incomplete attention to risks in studies simulating the pressure one would feel at 30,000 above sea level (Hilts & Stolberg, 1999). So if you look at the guidelines developed by the Department of Health and Human Services (HSS), you will see that much of it appears irrelevant to a great deal of psychological research.

Nonetheless, researchers are obligated to follow the regulations designed to protect research participants from harm as they participate in research. Even though your research is quite innocuous, you still need to attend to the regulations. In addition, if you are a member or student member of APA, you must follow APA's ethical standards; if you do not, you may be subject to sanctions such as expulsion from the association.

(In some of the guidelines, you will see people referred to as *subjects*; in other places, they are called *participants*. The two terms are largely interchangeable in research with people. APA has reversed a stricture that encouraged the use of *participants* rather than *subjects* because many researchers were aggravated by APA's policy.)

What Constitutes Research?

The question of what constitutes research seems as if it should have an obvious answer. Even so, the federal government in the United States has specified what qualifies as research for the purpose of protecting people.

HHS has generated a specific definition of what constitutes research. It is "a systematic investigation, including research development, testing and evaluation, designed to develop or contribute to generalizable knowledge" (Code of Federal Regulations, 2010, para. 46.102[d]).

In the context of evaluating whether a project constitutes research, HHS has generated a flowchart to help determine if a project is covered by its guidelines. The flowchart appears in Figure 3.1 and is available online at www.hhs.gov/ohrp/policy/checklists/decisioncharts.html.

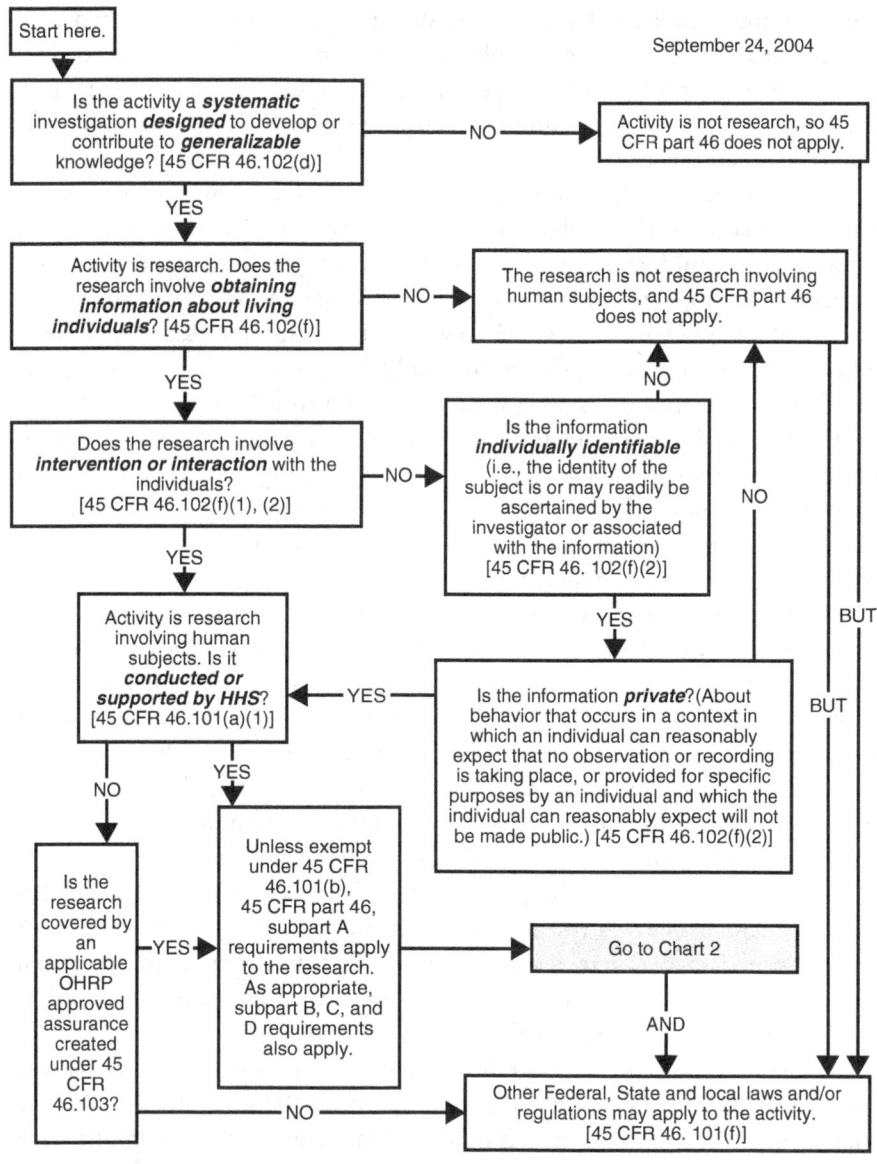

Figure 3.1   Flowchart to determine if a project constitutes research as defined by the U.S. Department of Health and Human Services.

Source: U.S. Department of Health & Human Resources.

This way of differentiating research and nonresearch may have implications for you. For example, one of the questions that you would answer in using the flowchart is "Does the research involve intervention or interaction with the individuals?" If you are conducting observational research in a public area and are not manipulating any variables but only recording behaviors of people in that area, your project would not constitute research according to federal guidelines. As such, you would not need specific approval to conduct it.

On the other hand, if you were doing a study in which you manipulated a variable in that public area, your study would constitute research because you would be using an intervention or maybe interacting with your subjects. The important point here is that you have to pay attention to the details of the guidelines so you know how to plan your research project. Most research you are likely to do would be considered research by the HHS guidelines, but you need to check to make sure.

The reason for the guidelines is ultimately to protect research participants from harm. As I noted above, most psychological research is fairly free of risk issues. But if your work constitutes research, you need to let an official committee review it to make sure that your participants are not likely to be exposed to experience adverse outcomes.

Every college and university where research takes place is required to have an Institutional Review Board (IRB) that scrutinizes research proposals to see if there are potential adverse effects on participants. The IRB assesses the potential risks in light of the potential benefits. The IRB might determine that there is significant likelihood that there will be some level of harm to participants, or the IRB might determine that harm might be unlikely, but that if it occurs, it will be significant. In either case, the IRB might decide that the research shouldn't be carried out.

On the other hand, if the potential benefits are considerable, the IRB might conclude that the research is worth doing, even if the likelihood of some harm is high. There is a trade-off in such decisions. If the potential risk is greater than the potential benefit, the study will not be approved. If the benefit is great, the IRB will approve the study.

In most psychological research, the benefits are slight, but so are the risks. In biomedical research, the benefits might be considerable, but so might the risks. For example, a new treatment for a disease might have notable benefit for the research participant—a cure. But because you never really know the actual outcome of a proposed study, the risk might be great—less relief from distress compared to an existing drug or even severe negative reaction to the new drug.

The criteria that an IRB uses to make its decision sound straightforward. But judgment calls are always part of the process. It is the IRB's role to make such judgments.

Understanding the Concept of Risk in Research

The IRB makes its assessment of the risk and benefit before the research actually takes place, which means that the IRB has to deal with probabilities and estimates about what is likely to happen. This assessment is not foolproof. The IRB can only make its best judgment about risk and benefit.

According to HHS, there are several kinds of harm that can result from research participation. If any harm results, the most likely types are either psychological or physical pain. Other less likely types include legal harm, social harm, and economic harm. Matching each type of potential harm is a corresponding potential benefit, such as psychological or physical benefits (Belmont Report, 1979, para. C-2).

Much psychological research entails what HHS refers to as *minimal risk*. Minimal-risk research would involve harm that would not exceed what you would expect to occur in everyday life. When a study falls into this category, it requires less stringent oversight than research entailing greater levels of potential harm (Code of Federal Regulations, 2010, para. 46.102 [i]).

What Research Requires Prior Approval?

As noted above, any activity that falls into the category of research has to undergo scrutiny by an IRB before the work can begin. How can you tell if your research requires IRB approval? One way is to look at the decision flowchart that HHS has developed, which appears in Figure 3.1.

As you can figure out from the chart, most research you plan will require IRB approval according to federal regulation. In addition, there may be state laws that govern research with people that go beyond the federal regulations. Obviously, you are obligated to follow those laws too.

In some cases, your research may be eligible for expedited review. This type of review typically involves an assessment of research by a subcommittee of the IRB and can take place outside of the board's normally scheduled meetings.

How can you tell if your project is appropriate for expedited review? Generally, if your project involves minimal risk, as described above, expedited review may be possible. Or if your work is a continuation of previously approved research, you may be able to use expedited review. HHS has provided a decision flowchart to help you figure out whether expedited review makes sense for your project. You can see the flowchart in Figure 3.2. All flowcharts related to the IRB approval are available online at www.hhs.gov/ohrp/policy/checklists/decisioncharts.html.

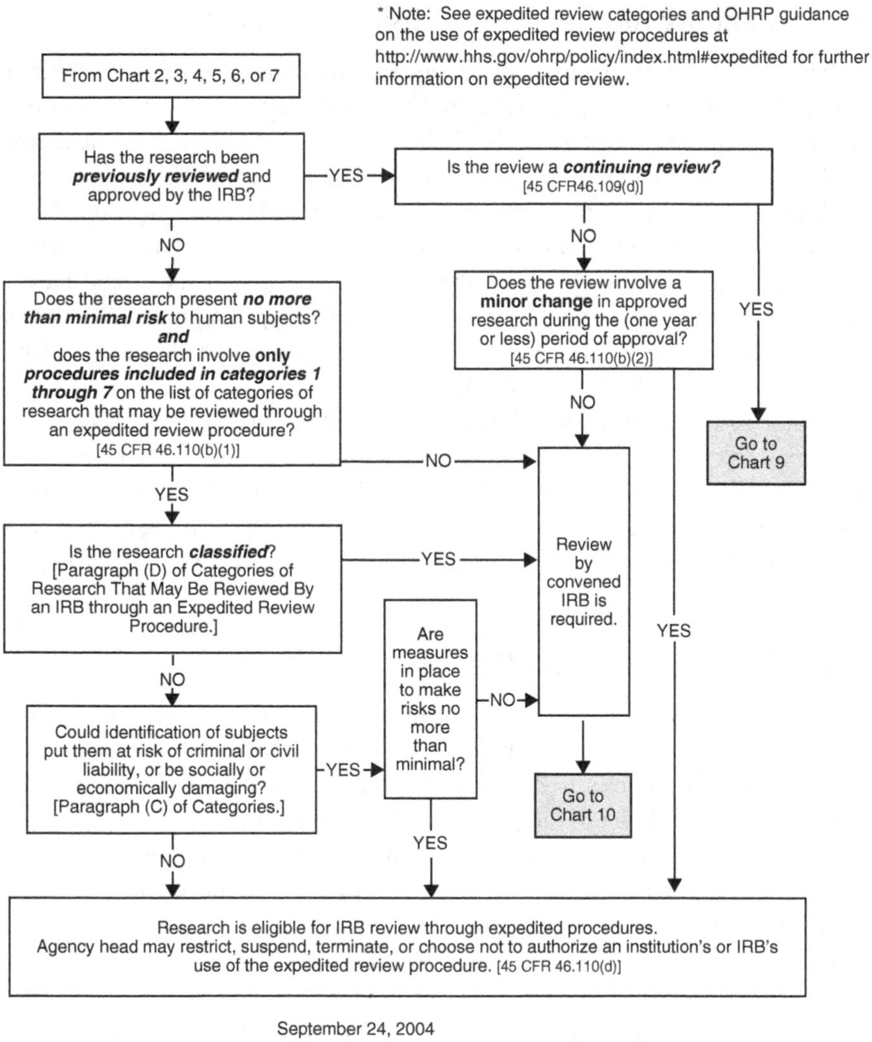

Figure 3.2   Flowchart to determine if a project constitutes research as defined by the U.S. Department of Health and Human Services.

Source: U.S. Department of Health & Human Resources.

Important Ethical Issues in Psychological Research

Some components of psychological research merit specific attention because they are either universal across studies or because they appear frequently in psychological research. The information in this section overlaps with what you have already read, but because it is relevant to a great deal of psychological research, I am repeating it here.

Informed Consent

One of the fundamental ethical principles is that people need to have information to decide whether they want to participate in research. One way to ensure that they have the information they need is through the informed consent process.

When you recruit participants, you should tell them what the research involves. This does not mean that you have to give them every detail about the study. They probably would not want to know every last detail anyway. But you should tell them how long the study will last, what they will be doing, and you should inform them about any significant likelihood of harm.

Another important aspect of their participation is that they have the right to decline participation without penalty and to withdraw from the study at any time. Researchers (and ethicists) recognize that participation must be voluntary if it is to be ethical. You also need to tell potential subjects that their data will be kept confidential. You should also tell them of any inducement for taking part in the study; for much psychological research, this entails extra credit in a class. In some instances, if a researcher has grant money, participants may be paid; they need to know about this in advance too.

In laboratory-based research, it is typical for participants to complete an informed consent form. The investigator is sometimes mandated to keep the signed form for some period of time. For online research, however, you cannot get a signed informed consent form from participants. There are different ways of dealing with this, one of which is to require the participants to actively respond that they have read the informed consent form and that they agree with its provisions.

Deception

Deception in psychological research is a fact of life. Some psychologists believe that it is highly undesirable (e.g., Hertwig & Ortmann, 2008; Ortmann & Hertwig, 1997), but others have argued that participants understand that possible deception is an acceptable element of research (e.g., Korn, 1998). Part of the argument also depends on how you define deception (Bröder, 1998). Nonetheless, deception is an element in over 40% of recent social psychological studies that have appeared in two prominent journals,

Journal of Personality and Social Psychology and *Journal of Experimental Social Psychology* (Hertwig & Ortmann, 2008).

What constitutes deception can involve judgment calls. For example, you may not tell a participant every single detail about a study because some details are irrelevant to risk issues and the person may not want to know all the details. You need to decide if the details that you omit are germane to ethical issues. If not, you are not deceiving people; rather, you are simply not telling them everything about your study. On the other hand, there is active deception, which is simply called *lying* in everyday life. This is the type of deception that causes the controversies.

APA has declared that researchers should avoid active deception whenever possible. If you can address your research question by using methodology free of deception, you should do so.

Debriefing

Once you have completed a testing session with participants, you should inform them of the important elements of the study, including its purpose and any deception that was involved. Furthermore, you need to clear up any misconceptions that you may have generated.

In rare instances, participation in a research project may lead to a negative emotional state. For example, a person who cannot solve difficult puzzles in an experiment may be unhappy with the outcome. It is the researcher's role to make sure that the person is not in a negative mood when leaving the laboratory. In rare instances, like Stanley Milgram's obedience research, compensatory follow-up should occur. This involves contacting the person later to find out if the adverse reaction has persisted and taking steps to remedy the situation as needed. The vast majority of research does not require compensatory follow-up.

Preparing for Evaluation by Your Institutional Review Board

Your IRB needs to have certain kinds of information in order to evaluate your proposal. Every institution has its own specific form, but the questions that a prospective researcher needs to address are fairly similar in many cases.

The first determination that you will make is whether your research is exempt from review, is eligible for expedited review, or requires full review. You can tell the IRB what you have concluded, and they will evaluate your request. A study can be exempt from review if it is observational research in a public space, if it is a study of educational practices, or if it meets other criteria established by HHS. The IRB needs to document that such research does not require review.

Expedited review is appropriate for continuing research that involves minimal risk. So if you are part of a laboratory that has done other research related to yours, your project may be appropriate for expedited review. Or if your plan to conduct survey research on nonsensitive topics, it could go through expedited review.

Other types of research require review by the full board. You can check with a researcher who is familiar with the policies in your institution or with your IRB for specific details, which may vary across schools.

Commonly Requested Information for IRB Proposals

Description of the Project

Frequently, an IRB form starts with an overall description of the research. It is generally quite brief and is designed to give members of the IRB a general sense of the nature of the research. At my institution, the IRB provides space for approximately 250 words for this description. Your institution may permit somewhat longer and more detailed opening descriptions.

Because the IRB consists of people who are not researchers, you should provide an abstract of your research that a well-educated person would comprehend, even if the person was not well versed in psychological research. The committee is likely to want a description of who you intend to recruit and how you will recruit them, what activity they will experience, and perhaps the objectives of the research.

Participants

The IRB may be interested in the nature of your subjects. This can be an important element of the evaluation because some groups of people are considered vulnerable, that is, they could be taken advantage of or they may be susceptible to harm that other groups are not. Such groups include children, people with developmental disabilities, prisoners, and pregnant women.

Much psychological research makes use of college students. One important factor here is that people under the age of 18 are not legally empowered to make decisions about participation; according to the law, participation requires parental consent. So if you are going to recruit from introductory psychology classes that contain first-year students, you have to let such students know that they may not sign up for or participate in your project.

Risks and Benefits of Participation

The IRB will pay close attention to your statement of risk. As I have stressed several times, most psychological research does not involve much risk at all. If other researchers have conducted research similar to yours, it may be wise to indicate that the procedure you will use is an established approach to the research question. If other researchers have taken your approach without adverse reactions by their participants, the IRB may be reassured that the risks associated with the methodology are negligible.

In the event that there are risks, you should specify how you will deal with them. If you planned to induce a temporary, negative mood in your participants, you would want to specify how you would ensure that the participants left the lab in a good mood, perhaps by having them rate a series of jokes. Or if you provided false feedback on performance, indicating that the subjects performed extremely poorly (when, in fact, they had not), you could specify that you would debrief the subjects completely and provide them with a task that they could complete, thus reassuring the subjects that there were hidden difficulties with the task you gave them.

Anonymity and Confidentiality of Participation

Your participants should know that you will not share their data with anybody outside your research team. In addition, you should point this fact out to the IRB. Ideally, there would be no way to connect any single person's data with that person specifically. However, this constraint is not possible if your participants are going to return for a later session and you need to be able to link their early behavior with later behavior.

The difference between anonymity and confidentiality is that with anonymity nobody knows who has participated. If you test a group of people, anonymity is not possible. Most of the time, this is not really a concern. It becomes quite important, though, if somebody is participating in research on sensitive issues (e.g., sexual behavior or criminal activity) or on therapy.

In contrast, confidentiality involves the inability to connect a person's responses in the research to the person individually. In most research, confidentiality will suffice; anonymity is not crucial. If the study does not involve anything controversial, people will not be concerned that others know that they participated. You should make sure, though, that nobody could be embarrassed or exposed to other psychological harm due to the fact that somebody knows how they responded during the study.

Chapter 4

Adapting and Developing Your Methodology

Making Use of Previous Research

It is easy to imagine that you might develop a research project that would be so unusual and lead to such dramatic results that everybody would recognize it as being as revolutionary as you would hope it is. Unfortunately, that virtually never happens. Just about every research project is the product of previous research and advances our knowledge a small step beyond what we already know or corrects a small misunderstanding that has arisen.

If you read just about any journal article, you will see that it invariably cites previous research. In fact, it is not unusual for a journal article to refer to 50 or more previous publications. Each of those citations brings in information that helped the researchers formulate their ideas and will help readers understand how the ideas for the journal article developed.

For instance, Svaldi, Zimmermann, and Naumann (2012) investigated the relation between self-esteem and body image. The rationale for their procedure was clear; it arose from earlier research on the same topic, body image, self-esteem, and the potential for eating disorders. Meijboom, Jansen, Kampman, and Schouten (1999) had studied self-esteem among restrained eaters, people who are always watching what they eat or who generally restrict what they do eat. Meijboom et al. reported that low self-esteem was associated with body shape and weight in restrained eaters, but only in tasks that did not involve conscious thoughts about self-esteem. That is, the relation between these constructs only became apparent when the researchers used a subliminal task related to self-esteem.

With this result in mind, Svaldi et al. (2012) decided to use a subliminal task in their research, which differed from that of Meijboom et al. (1999) in that Svaldi et al. did not explore the concept of restrained eating. Rather, they investigated whether there was a link between self-esteem and level of body dissatisfaction. Thus, Svaldi et al. relied on the results from the previous study for their research and borrowed some of the methodology from that research.

Svaldi et al. (2012) measured participants' level of body dissatisfaction and then experimentally manipulated participants' self-esteem by presenting the pronoun *I* paired either with positive adjectives like *good* or *valuable* or negative adjectives like *lousy* and *worthless*. The investigators set up the presentation format so that the stimuli were visible for only 60 milliseconds (i.e., 60 thousandths of a second) and were followed by a string of random letters; this procedure ensured that the participants would not consciously be aware of the words.

The participants thought that the research involved a vigilance task and that they had only to identify the location of what appeared to be flashes of light on a screen. The next step in the experiment involved having participants write down their current thoughts of themselves for 3 minutes; later, participants looked at themselves in a mirror for 1 minute.

Finally, the participants rated how positively or negatively they viewed individual letters of the alphabet. The researchers then analyzed the ratings of letters associated with the initials of the participants' names. The participants also completed an inventory of self-esteem.

The researchers used this approach for specific reasons. First, the point of the study was based on the results of previous research and on theory. In addition, the methodology involved components that a number of different researchers had already used successfully. Table 4.1 shows how the researchers used the work of others to create their study.

As you can see in the table, the research by Svaldi et al. (2012) relied on materials and procedures that others had developed. There was nothing new in this research regarding the individual measurements and procedures;

what was new about the research by Svaldi et al. was how they combined the ideas of others into a new set of research questions. The list of references shows how important the work of previous investigators can be to the development of new ideas.

Table 4.1   Procedures That Svaldi, Zimmermann, and Naumann (2012) Used, Why They Used Them, and the Sources That Provided Guidance for the Research

Procedure	Why They Used It	Relevant Sources They Cited
Viewing oneself in a mirror generates self-schemas about the body.	1. Viewing the body can trigger emotions regarding one's satisfaction with the body. 2. Cognitive theory predicts that contexts like looking at oneself in a mirror trigger body-schemas.	Cooper, Taylor, Cooper, and Fairburn (1987) Williamson, Muller, Reas, and Thaw (1999)
Body Shape Questionnaire	This instrument measures level of body dissatisfaction.	Hoffmeister, Teige-Mocigemba, Blechert, Klauer, and Tuschen-Caffier (2010)
Rosenberg Self-Esteem Scale	This inventory measures self-esteem and has been used successfully in a lot of previous research.	Blaskovich and Tomaka (1991) Ferring and Filipp (1996) Rosenberg (1965, 1979) Sinclair et al. (2010)
Name-Letter Task	This task indicates positive or negative valence of the letters constituting the initials in a person's name and reflects one's self-evaluation.	Greenwald and Banaji (1995) Kitayama and Karasawa (1997) LeBel and Gawronski (2009) Nuttin (1985, 1987)
Implicit Measure of Self-Esteem	This procedure affects self-esteem by pairing the pronoun *I* with either positive or negative adjectives.	Riketta and Dauenheimer (2003)
Three-minute period of self-reflection	This procedure affects explicit measures of self-esteem that follow implicit manipulations.	Grumm, Nestler, and von Collani (2009)

After reaching a conclusion, researchers try to figure out the next step in their research. It is never the case that you end up with a final body of knowledge. There is always more to be learned, always another research project to undertake. So what did Svaldi et al. (2012) suggest regarding future research?

They noted that participants in the high body dissatisfaction group did not experience a change in self-esteem after the positive self-esteem manipulation. This may have been due to the fact that the positive self-esteem manipulation raised their self-concept, but viewing themselves in the mirror may have brought it down again. Thus, the experimenters suggested that a control condition not involving a mirror might be a good next step.

These researchers also suggested a study involving monitoring eye movements to see how different participants move their eyes as they look at themselves in the mirror. Obviously, this type of manipulation would involve some sophisticated technology, but the concept illustrates how researchers develop new ideas based on the results of research projects. Furthermore, Svaldi et al. (2012) did not obtain a premanipulation measure of body dissatisfaction to guarantee that the participants in the high and low body dissatisfaction began the study with comparable levels of body dissatisfaction.

If you were to generate a study comparable to that of Svaldi et al. (2012), you would need to have software that could present stimuli for brief periods and in different locations on a computer screen. Although such software is not available everywhere, it is relatively inexpensive, so departmental budgets could potentially accommodate the software.

In addition, it is possible to generate research questions that do not require unusual software or instrumentation. For example, you read in Chapter 3 about predictions of terror management theory and how people adjust to the fact that some day they will die. Researchers using the Disgust Scale (Haidt, McCauley, & Rozin, 1994; Olatunji et al., 2007) have shown that when people are reminded of their mortality, their ratings of disgust are elevated (Goldenberg et al., 2001).

In other, related research, Goldenberg, Pyszczynski, McCoy, Greenberg, and Solomon (1999) reported that people scoring high in neuroticism thought of death when primed with thoughts of the physical aspects of sex. So there are likely to be interesting research questions involving aspects of disgust, personality variables, and thoughts of death.

Just as Dietz, Albowicz, and Beins (2011) combined humor, personality, and predictions of terror management theory, it might be productive to explore personality, disgust, and terror management theory. Such research would be relatively easy to pursue. You could use the Disgust Scale with its 25 disgust-relevant statements (e.g., *You are walking barefoot on concrete and step on an earthworm*) and personality inventories such as those made available by the Oregon Research Institute International Personality Item Pool (http://ipip.ori.org) to find any relations among variables.

Goldenberg et al. (1999) found that participants high in neuroticism differed from those low in neuroticism in susceptibility to thoughts of death when primed with physical aspects of sex. Perhaps when primed with disgust, those scoring high in neuroticism would be more inclined to think of death than those low in neuroticism. Such research is feasible and practical. It involves an interesting psychological question and could produce striking results.

To create such a study, you would need to familiarize yourself with the basics of terror management theory, perhaps by reading the research of Goldenberg and her colleagues (1999, 2001). In addition, you would find out how different personality characteristics might be associated with disgust, thoughts of death, and so forth. Then you could prime participants with disgusting stimuli and see how they respond.

Borrowing From Previous Research

If you are doing a research project that you are creating, you might ask yourself why you would borrow from previous research. After all, if you are going to create new knowledge, shouldn't you use new methods? There are some very good reasons for adapting stimuli and procedures from other researchers. As long as you give appropriate credit to the other researchers for the foundation they laid, it is entirely acceptable to use somebody else's ideas. In addition, it will likely save you a lot of time.

One important issue is that developing an entirely new methodology is not easy. It can take considerable preparatory work before a new approach is ready for use in an actual study. Here are some examples of existing inventories that psychologists have generated and that you could use for your research project.

Multidimensional Sense of Humor Scale

Thorson and Powell (1993a, 1993b) wanted to create an inventory to measure the sense of humor. To do this, they had to figure out what really constitutes the sense of humor. They determined that an adequate measure would involve several different dimensions, an approach that differed from previous attempts at such measurement.

When they did their work, several psychologists had already developed scales to measure the sense of humor, but Thorson and Powell believed that the earlier scales did not focus on the constructs that they thought were most important. For example, Martin and Lefcourt (1984) developed the Situational Humor Response Questionnaire (SHRQ) so they could obtain information from people about humor in everyday situations. Like Thorson and Powell (1993a, 1993b), Martin and Lefcourt had believed that they could develop a different measurement scale that would remedy deficiencies in past attempts, such as the IPAT Humor Test of Personality (Tollefson & Cattell, 1963).

But Thorson and Powell (1993a) identified several potential dimensions to the sense of humor, such as the following:

- Recognition of oneself as a humorous person based on past successes and failures in dealing with humorous situations
- Recognition of the humor produced by others, that is, the ability to "get the joke"
- Appreciation of humor and attitudes toward people who use humor
- Laughter as a behavior that indicates actual humor recognition
- Perspective that includes an outlook reflecting an acceptance of humor
- Coping as an adaptive mechanism that accepts a negative situation by conjuring up humor that could be related to it, including so-called gallows humor

So they created an inventory that would tap into these different dimensions. But it was not a quick or easy task. They initially generated about 20 statements that they believed could pertain to each of the dimensions of humor they identified. The initial pool of items consisted of 124 statements. They asked 264 people (students and members of a local civic club) to respond to the statement on a 5-point scale of *strongly disagree* to *strongly agree* that a statement described them. The statements included the following examples: *My clever sayings amuse others* and *Uses of humor help put me at ease* (Thorson & Powell, 1993a, p. 21).

After testing their initial sample, they used a statistical approach called factor analysis to see how the various statements grouped together. There were 22 items that met the criterion they established for inclusion in the set. Then they added eight more items that they had previously discarded and analyzed this set. Finally, they generated a 24-item inventory, which they named the Multidimensional Sense of Humor Scale, and tested it on a sample of 426 people.

The result is now that psychologists have a reliable scale that appears to measure the construct of sense of humor. My students and I have used it for several different studies (e.g., Beins & O'Toole, 2010; Doychak, Herschman, Ferrante, & Beins, 2012; Ippolito & Beins, 2011). Fortunately for us, Thorson and Powell (1993a, 1993b) did the hard work of creating the scale and testing over 700 people to develop and validate it.

As you can see, it is much easier to use an existing inventory, whether it be for measuring sense of humor or personality characteristics, than to have to create your own. Thinking back on Thorson and Powell's (1993b) inventory, if you imagine trying to identify the dimensions of the sense of humor, then coming up with questions that will (or, maybe, will not) successfully tap into those dimensions, then analyzing your data, then repeating the whole process until you are satisfied that you have what you want, it can be a long and drawn out process.

Rather than creating your own measurement device, you can instead go to page 801 of Thorson and Powell's (1993b) journal article and use the 24 items they created.

Ambivalent Sexism Inventory and Ambivalence Toward Men Inventory

Similarly, if you want to assess participants' levels of sexism toward women, you could use the Ambivalent Sexism Inventory that Glick and Fiske (1996) created. (It's on page 512 of their journal article.) If you wanted to measure sexism toward men, you could use the Ambivalence Toward Men Inventory that Glick and Fiske (1999) created. (It's on page 536 of their journal article.) These authors request that researchers contact them for permission to use the inventories, but they have been gracious in the past in granting permission.

Measures of Personality and Social Psychology

Additional measures of psychological characteristics abound. For example, Robinson, Shaver, and Wrightsman (1991) compiled an entire book that consists of nothing but measures of social psychology and personality. Table 4.2 lists the chapters and titles of some of the inventories. It almost seems that you can find any characteristic you would like to measure.

Various Personality Characteristics

The Oregon Research Institute (ORI) has a collaboratory that has created 269 personality scales. The ORI has made the scales available for researchers without cost. The personality traits that are available range from achievement striving (e.g., *Go straight for the goal*) to zest (e.g., *Look forward to each new day*).

Table 4.2   Sample of Scales in Measures of Personality and Social
Psychological Attitudes

Chapter	Example of Scale
Measurement and Control of Response Bias	CPI[a] Good Impression Scale
Measures of Subjective Well-Being	Life Satisfaction Scales
Measures of Self-Esteem	Rosenberg's Self-Esteem Scale
Social Anxiety, Shyness, and Related Constructs	Embarrassability Scale
Measures of Depression and Loneliness	Depressive Experiences Questionnaire
Alienation and Anomie	Powerlessness
Interpersonal Trust and Attitudes Toward Human Nature	Faith in People Scale
Locus of Control	Mental Health Locus of Control Scale
Authoritarianism and Related Constructs	Ethnocentrism Scale
Sex Roles: The Measurement of Masculinity, Femininity, and Androgyny	Sex Role Behavior Scale
Values	The Value Survey

Source: Robinson, Shaver, and Wrightsman (1991).
Note: Each chapter contains multiple scales.
[a]*CPI* = California Psychological Inventory

They are typically either 10- or 20-item inventories that you can use in your own research. Furthermore, the inventories have some reliability indices associated with them. For example, the four achievement-striving inventories have reliabilities as reflected in alpha coefficients of .78, .78, .79, and .82, which are respectable values for 10-item inventories.

In general, longer inventories have higher reliability values. For instance, one 10-item conscientiousness scale has an alpha coefficient of .81. Its 20-item counterpart has an alpha coefficient of .90. Normally, you would choose the longer inventory with its higher reliability index, but if your study is getting long, the 10-item version might make more sense. If you were correlating scores on inventories for the Big Five personality traits, using the 20-item version, your participants would have to respond to 100 items. If, in addition, you were assessing sexism toward men and toward women, your participants would be responding to 44 more items. And if you completed your study with the Multidimensional Sense of Humor Scale, it would add 24 more items. Such a study would involve 168 statements to which your participants would have to respond.

If your participants took 10 seconds per item, the study would last 28 minutes. If you wanted to add more tasks, a research session would be over half an hour. This length may seem inordinate to participants. You don't want to tax their patience because they might stop paying attention to the items, rushing through them, so their responses to the final scales might lack validity. By using the shorter versions of the personality inventories, you would take the duration down to about 20 minutes. Such practical considerations are important. There is no best way to lay out your study, but you need to rely on your judgment and experience (or the judgment and experience of your professors) to guide your choices.

Defining and Measuring Your Concepts and Constructs

When you read research reports, it often seems that the investigators took the approaches they did because it simply made sense to do so. But there are many different ways any given study could proceed. Researchers always have to make decisions about methodology and, subsequently, what statistics to use to analyze their data.

The most common way of proceeding is simply to follow in the footsteps of previous researchers, using their approach. This is a reasonable strategy because if it worked for them, it might work for you too.

However, sometimes you may want to create a different methodology to address a question. In such an instance, you can develop a different operational definition of your construct. For example, Thorson and Powell (1993a) operationalized *sense of humor* as a set of scores based on their Multidimensional Sense of Humor Scale. It might have been easier to use a previous instrument, like Martin and Lefcourt's (1984) Situational Humor Response Scale, but they believed that they needed to measure other aspects of humor appreciation.

Similarly, in an experiment on aggression, Lieberman, Solomon, Greenberg, and McGregor (1999) developed a new operational definition of aggression to overcome limitations of previous measurements. For example, in some research, participants undergo an experimental manipulation designed to generate an aggressive response, and then they make verbal statements or written comments that the researchers assess for evidence of an aggressive reaction (Berkowitz, 1970); unfortunately, a verbal statement is not the same as physical aggressiveness.

Other research has made use of electric shocks as a manifestation of aggressiveness. Lieberman et al. (1999) have noted several drawbacks with this methodology. First, it requires special instrumentation that may be expensive or unavailable; second, it involves an element of risk that an Institutional Review Board must assess and might not approve; third, participants may know that in Stanley Milgram's obedience experiments with ostensible shocks, no shocks were actually delivered, so they may believe that to be the case in a given study on aggressiveness; and fourth, the way studies have been set up, administering shocks may have represented something other than aggressiveness.

With these drawbacks in mind, Lieberman et al. (1999) used a "hot sauce paradigm." They assigned participants either to a condition in which they were reminded that someday they would die or to a neutral, non-death-related condition. In each condition, half the participants read an essay that that they agreed with and half read an essay that they disagreed with.

Participants in the study were later asked to determine the amount of very hot sauce to give to a supposed participant who wrote the essay they had just read and who would have to drink the hot sauce. The researchers measured the weight of the hot sauce (which nobody actually drank) to get a measurement of aggressive behavior: the greater the weight, the greater the level of aggression.

Lieberman et al. (1999) predicted that when reminded of their ultimate death, participants would administer more hot sauce to the supposed writer of the essay when it presented a perspective that conflicted with that of the participants. The results revealed that when reminded of death, which is anxiety provoking, participants acted more harshly (i.e., administered more hot sauce) toward the writer of an essay with which they disagreed. The study involved a new method of measuring aggression that eliminated some of the weaknesses of other methods.

When a new and useful approach appears, others may make use of it as well. For example, Adachi and Willoughby (2011) investigated the extent to which video games led to aggressive behavior. After having been exposed to competitive and violent video games, the researchers let players administer hot sauce to another person in what was purported to be a taste preference study. The results indicated no effect of violence in the video games, but when a game involved competition, the allocation of hot sauce was greater than for games that were not competitive in nature.

In experimental research with a related focus, Brummert Lennings and Warburton (2011) found that participants who had listened to music with violent lyrics administered more hot sauce to others than did people who had not listened to such music.

The development of the measurement of aggressiveness by measuring hot sauce (Lieberman et al., 1999) is a good example of how researchers identify limitations in the methodology that preceded them and improved on it. The studies on video games (Adachi & Willoughby, 2011) and on violence in music (Brummert Lennings & Warburton, 2011) are good examples of how researchers borrow techniques that others have successfully developed and used.

By measuring the amount of hot sauce that one person would give to another, we can operationally define aggressiveness in a way that has advantages over previous measurements such as evaluating written statements that have aggressive themes or delivering shocks. Furthermore, the ethical issue of actually making another person suffer, even if only mildly, is not relevant here.

Identifying Your Research Participants

Once you have decided on your methodology and received approval from your Institutional Review Board, you can begin data collection. The next issue that you need to resolve is the nature of your research participants. Psychologists virtually never use probabilistic, random samples. Rather, we rely on convenience samples most of the time. These are frequently groups of students who receive extra credit in psychology classes.

There are some ways to expand your sample beyond students. For example, for a relatively small amount of money, you can use the so-called Mechanical Turk that Amazon.com has created for researchers. If you have a short study, you can pay people a small amount of money (e.g., a quarter) to participate in your study. The sample still isn't random, but it can be broad. You can also consider using the Psychological Research on the Net page that Hanover College sponsors (http://psych.hanover.edu/research/exponnet.html). This website lists quite a large number of ongoing studies; yours could be one of them. Again, the sample will not be random, but it will likely be broader than the typical convenience sample of students.

How Many Participants Do You Need?

The short answer to the question regarding sample size is that you should use as many participants as you can. Naturally, though, nothing in research is as simple as that. One general rule that researchers use is that you should have at least 30 participants per group. The rationale for this value is that your data are likely to be approximately normally distributed when you have 30 observations; normality is desirable for many of the statistical tests we use.

However, an effective sample size differs depending on the characteristics of your research. In order to spot a significant difference between groups, which is the goal of many projects, you want to maximize the statistical power of your analysis. That is, you want to be able to reject the null hypothesis when you should.

There are a couple of principles related to the sample size in this regard. Let's assume that your experimental manipulation really leads to a reliable effect. If your sample consists of people who are quite different to begin with, you will need a large sample to spot your reliable effect. If you compare two groups, and each consists of people whose scores on your dependent variable are all over the place to begin with, it is hard to detect the effect of an experimental manipulation because there is so much variability to begin with. The additional difference due to your manipulation may not be all that apparent. When populations are fairly homogeneous to begin with, you need a smaller sample size in order to spot differences between groups.

As you can see in Figure 4.1, when variances of population are large, it is possible for scores to differ greatly within a single group, so the mean of a sample could be high or it could be low. The higher mean would not reflect the result of an experimental manipulation; it would only reflect natural variability of scores. So if you tested participants in two groups that had high variability, you wouldn't know if your differences were due to a treatment effect or to natural variability. On the other hand, when there is little variability within each population, two means that show the same size difference as you saw on the left side of Figure 4.1 would probably be attributable to an experimental treatment, not to natural variability because there isn't much natural variability.

A second consideration in selecting your sample size is the magnitude of the effect of your experimental manipulation. If you expect that the experimental and control groups are likely to be quite different because your manipulation will have a great effect, you don't need as large a sample size as when the experimental manipulation is likely to have a small effect.

When you conduct a statistical analysis, you can spot real differences across groups either by using large groups, if the variability within a population is large, or smaller groups, if the natural variability is small. Similarly, with small effect sizes you want larger samples, and with large effects, you can get away with smaller samples. Published journal articles vary greatly in their sample sizes, but it is not unusual for investigators in laboratory studies to include well over 100 participants.

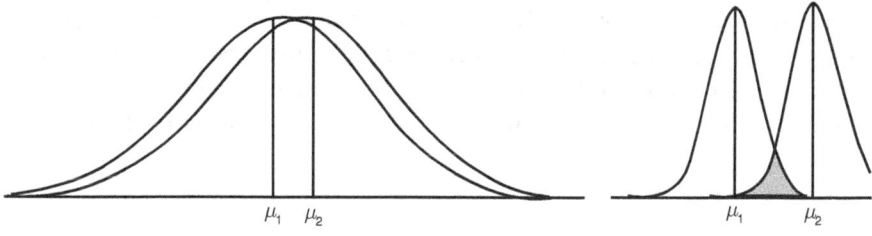

Figure 4.1	Illustration of how variability in a population can affect conclusions about mean differences. In the two situations above, mean differences are about the same, but in the figure on the left, it would be hard to tell if a difference in samples is due to a treatment or to natural variability. In the figure on the population, you need larger sample sizes to be confident that a difference is due to an experimental treatment rather than to natural variability among participants.

In general, larger sample sizes are more sensitive for detecting real differences between groups. If your sample size is too small, the lack of a statistically significant difference could be due to the lack of an effect of your experimental manipulation or it could be due to natural variability that is obscuring a real difference. The problem is that you don't know which is the case. So you should test as many participants as is practical for you. Getting guidance on variability and effect sizes from somebody who knows about the topic is always a good idea.

Do the Data Support Your Hypotheses? Planning for Your Data Analysis

Part of your research planning should include testing to see if your data support your hypotheses. One element of this is figuring out what such support would look like and what kind of data analysis will tell you if the support is reliable. You should identify the statistics that you are going to use before you begin your data collection, making sure that the statistics are appropriate for helping you answer your research question.

There are too many different methodologies to list them all. And there are too many statistical approaches to list easily. But there are some common methods and statistics that investigators turn to.

Comparing Means

If your research is experimental, with random assignment of participants to groups, or quasi-experimental, with groups based on pre-existing characteristics, you are likely to consider tests that examine differences between groups, usually differences between the means of the groups. Table 4.3 gives a basic look at statistical tests that many researchers use. New statistical approaches sometimes appear, so the tests in the table do not exhaust the possibilities.

Table 4.3   Methodological Approaches and Statistical Tests That Often Accompany Designs That Test for Differences Between Means

Methodology	Statistical Test
One independent variable with a comparison of means of two groups to see if the means differ	• Independent groups t test if there are different participants in each group *or* • Dependent groups (also called related groups or correlated groups) t test if you test the same participants in the two groups
One independent variable with a comparison of means of two or more groups to see if the means differ	• One-way analysis of variance (ANOVA) • When you have a significant F value: Post hoc comparisons to see which groups are significantly different If you used a repeated measures design, you would use a slightly different approach than if there are different participants in each group.
Multiple independent variables with a comparison of means of different groups on one independent variable at a time	• Factorial analysis of variance • When you have a significant F value: Post hoc comparisons to see which groups are significantly different. (You don't need post hoc tests if there are only two groups for a given independent variable.) If you used a repeated measures design, you would use a slightly different approach than if there are different participants in each group. Repeated measures designs involve issues that can be more complex than those for independent groups designs.

Establishing Relations Between Variables

Some research does not relate to differences between groups. Instead, such research examines whether variables are related to one another. For example, if you measure the constructs of risk taking and recklessness, you might want to know if people who score high on one also tend to score high on the other. It may not make sense to ask if people score higher on risk taking than on recklessness if you simply want to see if the two go together.

In addition, you might want to know if scores on the Disgust Scale (Olatunji et al., 2007) correlate with degree of neuroticism. Scores on the Disgust Scale can range from 0 to 100; scores on a scale of neuroticism might range from 0 to 50. It would not make sense to compare the means of the two because they are measured on different ranges of numbers. Besides, it isn't clear what it would mean if they did (or didn't) differ. Rather, you would probably be more interested in whether people who score high on one scale also score high on the other. This approach calls for correlational analysis.

The most common correlational statistic is the Pearson product-moment correlation. You may see writers commenting that this statistic is appropriate for scores on interval or ratio scale measurement. In reality, you can legitimately use the Pearson correlation even for scores on nominal and ordinal scales.

Alternate formulas that you sometimes see in statistics books are merely algebraic rearrangements of the formula for the Pearson correlation (Howell, 2007). So you can use formulas specific for ranked data (e.g., the Spearman correlation) or for nominal, dichotomous data (the phi coefficient), but you will get the same result as when you use the standard Pearson correlation formula. In fact, for ranked data, the Pearson formula is more accurate than the Spearman formula if there are tied ranks in the data (Howell, 2007, p. 286).

If you are interested in predicting the value of one variable based on another variable, you will likely use regression analysis. There are varieties of regression analyses, but the most common approach involves numbers on interval or ratio scales. So colleges and universities may predict how well a student will perform in classes during the first year in college (i.e., the student's grade-point average) based on SAT scores. (In reality, predictions will involve multiple variables, but if you understand the logic for predictions involving one variable, you will have a sense of how regression works for using multiple variables to make a prediction.)

For example, a student and I attempted to predict participants' ratings of jokes based on their scores on the Multidimensional Sense of Humor Scale (Benfante & Beins, 2007).

Based on our data, we predicted that if a person's sense of humor score was 4.0 (on a scale of 1 to 5), that person's average joke rating would have been 4.9 for the jokes we used. On the other hand, if the person's sense of humor score was 2.0, the average joke rating would be 3.4. These predictions were made on the basis of a linear regression formula, which is related to correlational analysis.

You can use one or multiple predictor variables in a regression analysis. This approach is typically used in correlational rather than experimental studies.

Chapter 5

Your Results

In this chapter you will learn about...

- ◆ Why Do We Use Statistics?
- ◆ What Is Your Message?
- ◆ Statistical Significance
- ◆ Deciding Whether the Results Supported Your Hypothesis
- ◆ Results Versus Interpretations

Why Do We Use Statistics?

Mark Twain popularized the saying that there are three kinds of lies: lies, damned lies, and statistics. It is no surprise that many people dislike statistics. Statistics involve numbers, which intimidate many people. In addition, people often don't really know why psychologists use statistics, which is simply as a tool to help us understand behavior.

In this chapter, I hope that you gain a better understanding of how to focus on the meaning of your research question as you present the results of your study. After all, the numbers are really secondary to the reason you carried out your research and are nothing more than a tool to help you arrive at an answer to your question. You have to know what statistics are appropriate for your study, but after that, they are often quite simple to use.

The purpose of your results section is to let others know how your participants behaved in your study. The most basic approach to statistics is the descriptive statistic. Just about everybody knows about the descriptive statistics associated with central tendency, even if they don't use those words. For example, to say that one group has a higher average than another group relies on descriptive statistics. There are different kinds of averages (e.g., mean, median, and mode), but all of them indicate what score is normal or typical.

Another type of descriptive statistic gives us a sense of how closely or widely spaced the values are in a group of numbers. The most common of these is the standard deviation. It is a less common term than *average*, but it isn't a complicated concept. Essentially, the standard deviation tells you how far from the average score a typical score is likely to fall. If the standard deviation is large, it means that it isn't unusual to find a score far from the mean; if the standard deviation is small, it means that a typical score falls close to the mean. There are several different measures of variability, but their purpose is to give you a sense of the spread of scores.

The second type of statistic is the inferential statistic. The general purpose of this type of statistic is to let you know if your results are reliable: That is, if you conduct your study again, are you likely to get the same results. When our findings are likely to be reliable, we say that they are significant. There are quite a few different inferential statistics, but their commonality is that they let you know about the reliability of your data.

If you understand what descriptive statistics tell you and if you understand what inferential statistics tell you, you know most of what you need in order to understand the statistics that psychologists use. This presentation is somewhat simplistic because some statistics are rather complex in usage, but the statistics you will probably use will not be all that complicated to understand.

What Is Your Message?

The key to presenting your research results is to tell your audience what you found as simply and clearly as possible. Naturally, if your study is complex, your presentation will have to reflect that complexity. But the first thing to do is to establish the main points you want to convey.

If your research involves comparing different groups to see if their means differ, your main point should simply be that when you compared the means, they differed or they didn't differ, depending on whether your inferential statistic is significant. If your research is correlational and is designed to assess whether variables are related to one another, you should simply say that the two variables are correlated or aren't correlated, depending on whether your correlations are significant.

In theory, if you had created a factorial design with two independent variables, your statement of results could be very short. Suppose that you had developed a 3 x 3 design with means as shown in Table 5.1. Hypothetically, your results section could be three sentences long. For instance, if you had one significant main effect and a significant interaction, you might simply say (a) that the difference between means on Variable A was significant and that the scores in the different groups were reliably different. Then you could say that (b) regarding Variable B, those groups were not reliably different. Then you could say that (c) there was a significant interaction, which means that in order to understand the results and to understand how your participants responded, you have to investigate the patterns of the different groups individually.

Naturally, you would actually want to say more than what I've given in the paragraph above, but those three brief sentences would give the reader the essence of your results. Again, hypothetically, you could present the results without any numbers or statistical tests. In practice, you would give more detail, but the important point here is that you should initially capture the important information in words that the reader will be able to comprehend. Then you can fill in the details with numbers and outcomes of any statistical tests you conduct.

To give you a sense of how you could actually develop the presentation of your results, consider some research that my students and I carried out. We developed a set of jokes that had different themes: death, sex, or neutral. Each of our participants rated one type of joke as to how funny they found each joke. Then we found the mean rating for each participant.

Table 5.1   Layout of 3 × 3 Factorial Design

| Levels of Variable B | Levels of Variable A | | | |
	A1	A2	A3	
B1	A1-B1	A2-B1	A3-B1	Overall mean of B1
B2	A1-B2	A2-B2	A3-B2	Overall mean of B2
B3	A1-B3	A2-B3	A3-B3	Overall mean of B3
	Overall mean of A1	Overall mean of A2	Overall mean of A3	

In addition, we measured the level of neuroticism of our participants using a scale from the International Personality Item Pool (http://ipip.ori. org) developed by the Oregon Research Institute. Based on these data, we categorized our participants as low, medium, or high in neuroticism.

Thus, we had a 3 × 3 design, reflecting our two independent variables (type of joke and level of neuroticism). Each variable had three levels. Various researchers have discovered that people high in neuroticism appreciate various types of jokes differently (e.g., Galloway & Chirico, 2008) and that people high in neuroticism respond to sexual ideas differently than people low in neuroticism (Goldenberg, Pyszczynski, McCoy, Greenberg, & Solomon, 1999).

So we investigated whether participants' ratings of jokes were related to their level of neuroticism and the themes of the jokes. It turned out that some interesting patterns of responses emerged (Dietz, Albowicz, & Beins, 2011). Here are the results:

First, we discovered that overall, level of neuroticism was not related to joke ratings. That is, participants scoring low, medium, and high on the neuroticism scale assigned the same overall ratings to jokes on a scale of 1 (*not funny*) to 7 (*very funny*). Second, there was a tendency for participants to prefer sex-related jokes, followed by neutral jokes, then death-related jokes.

However, the most interesting pattern was reflected in the interaction between the two variables. Low-neuroticism participants produced lower ratings of enjoyment for death-themed jokes and highest ratings for neutral jokes. On the other hand, the pattern for high-neuroticism participants differed. This group showed more enjoyment of sex- and death-themed jokes and least enjoyment of neutral jokes. Participants in the medium-neuroticism group tended to split the difference between the two extreme groups.

The material in the preceding two paragraphs provides a concise, accurate, and comprehensible description of the results. There are no numbers or statistical tests, just words that would make sense to just about anybody with a little background on the topic.

You wouldn't really want to be so concise in your research report because there are some details that put the ideas into perspective. Some of that detail involves simple descriptive statistics to accompany the paragraphs you just read. Take a look at the following paragraph, and you will see how you can introduce some of the descriptive statistics. I have indicated the new material with italics. (You wouldn't use italics in your presentation; I am simply doing it to show you the change.)

First, we discovered that overall, level of neuroticism was not related to joke ratings. That is, participants scoring low, medium, and high on the neuroticism scale assigned the same overall ratings to jokes on a scale of 1 (*not funny*) to

7 (*very funny*). *The means were 4.0, 3.9, and 3.9 for low, medium, and high neuroticism participants.* Second, there was a tendency for participants to prefer sex-related jokes, followed by neutral jokes, then death-related jokes. *The means were 4.2, 4.0, and 3.7, respectively.*

However, the most interesting pattern was reflected in the interaction between the two variables. Low-neuroticism participants produced lower ratings of enjoyment for death-themed jokes and highest ratings for neutral jokes. On the other hand, the pattern for high-neuroticism participants differed. This group showed more enjoyment of sex- and death-themed jokes and least enjoyment of neutral jokes. Participants in the medium-neuroticism group tended to split the difference between the two extreme groups.

The two paragraphs above are repetitions of the first presentation of the results with the addition of the averages for the various groups. The averages give a little more substance to the results.

One part of the presentation that would still benefit from some elaboration is the second paragraph, which introduces the interaction. Interactions are by definition more complex than the main effects of type of joke and level of participant neuroticism. The complexity of interactions arises because they involve consideration of multiple variables and combinations of groups at the same time.

In the example that we are considering here, some elaboration of the description of results is in order. One way to present an interaction is through a figure. If you look below, you can see how you might incorporate a graph to help get your point across. The first paragraph is the same as the one in the selection above, but the second paragraph refers to a figure that clarifies the situation. (The new material here is also in italics.)

First, we discovered that overall, level of neuroticism was not related to joke ratings. That is, participants scoring low, medium, and high on the neuroticism scale assigned the same overall ratings to jokes on a scale of 1 (*not funny*) to 7 (*very funny*). The means were 4.0, 3.9, and 3.9 for low, medium, and high neuroticism participants. Second, there was a tendency for participants to prefer sex-related jokes, followed by neutral jokes, then death-related jokes. The means were 4.2, 4.0, and 3.7, respectively.

However, the most interesting pattern was reflected in the interaction between the two variables. Low-neuroticism participants produced lower ratings of enjoyment for death-themed jokes and highest ratings for neutral jokes. On the other hand, the pattern for high-neuroticism participants differed. This group showed more enjoyment of sex- and death-themed jokes and least enjoyment of neutral jokes. Participants in the medium-neuroticism group tended to split the difference between the two extreme groups. *Figure 5.1 shows the relation between joke type and level of participant neuroticism.*

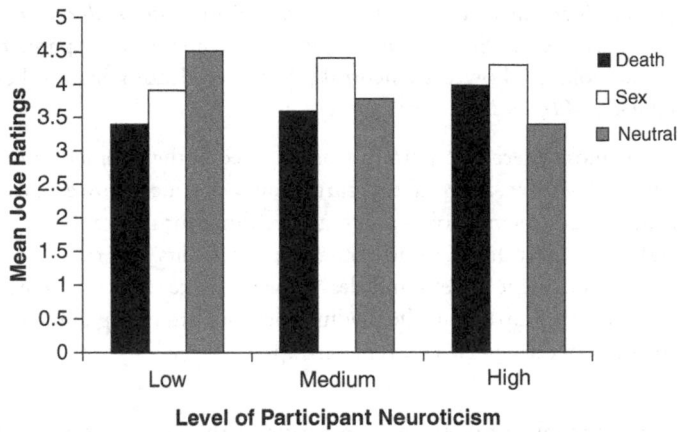

Figure 5.1   Ratings of jokes by joke type and level of participant neuroticism. Copyright 2012 Bernard C. Beins. Used with permission.

So now we have built up the presentation of the results starting with words to describe the outcome, then the addition of means, and now the inclusion of a figure. At each step, the numeric and graphic depictions help fill in the details, expanding on the basic message that you delivered verbally.

When you present your results in a figure, you have choices about formatting. For example, the same results that are depicted in Figure 5.1 appear in Figure 5.2. But in the second figure, different aspects of the data are highlighted. In the first figure, you can easily see the pattern of responses for

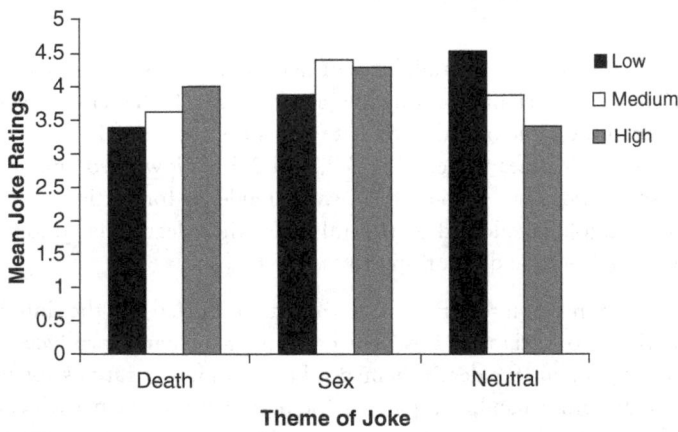

Figure 5.2   Ratings of jokes by joke type and level of participant neuroticism. Copyright 2012 Bernard C. Beins. Used with permission.

participants showing different levels of neuroticism. In the second figure, you can easily see the breakdown of results for ratings of different kinds of jokes. Your choice of layout will depend on what aspect of the results you want to highlight. Neither one is right or wrong; they are just different and will serve different purposes.

Instead of using a figure to present your data, you could create a table. Tables are not as visually arresting as graphs, but they present data more precisely. As you look at Figure 5.2, you can see the pattern of data quite easily, but you don't have exact values for the dependent variable. There is a trade-off in the use of a figure versus a table. A figure presents a coherent picture that is easy to digest; a table presents exact values that you can compare. Both are useful in their own ways. The data from Figures 5.1 and 5.2 appear in Table 5.2.

As a general rule, if you present material within your paragraphs, you don't need to repeat it in figures or in tables. Similarly, if you create graphs or tables, you don't include that information in the paragraphs. Whenever you use figures and tables, though, you should mention them in the text so the reader knows when to refer to that information. In printed journal articles, the tables and figures may not be on the same page as the verbal presentation that relates to them. So you are doing the reader a favor by indicating in the text when it is time to find relevant figures and tables.

One thing that you don't want to do is to simply list a string of numbers in the text. A long list of numbers has all the interest of reading a telephone book. If you have two or three means to present, your reader will be able to handle them if you list them in a sentence. But in the factorial design that I've used as an example here, you could list nine different mean values. After a few of them, the reader will stop paying attention because it gets hard to keep straight the relation between the groups and their means.

Table 5.2   Ratings of Jokes by Joke Type and Level of Participant Neuroticism

| Joke Theme | Neuroticism Level | | | |
	Low	Medium	High	
Death	3.4 (1.4)	3.6 (0.9)	4.0 (1.1)	(3.7)
Sex	3.9 (0.8)	4.4 (1.0)	4.3 (1.1)	(4.0)
Neutral	4.5 (1.1)	3.8 (0.8)	3.4 (0.8)	(4.2)
	(4.0)	(3.9)	(3.9)	

Note: Marginal means appear in parentheses. Standard deviations are in parentheses.

Statistical Significance

The presentation above gives a simple depiction of the results of our study. The results are fairly straightforward and relatively easy to understand. You can get the point without encountering overwhelming numbers or statistical tests, although as you have seen, adding some numerical information (i.e., descriptive statistics) helps fill in the details.

What we have not yet dealt with is the final aspect of the presentation of your results: results of statistical tests. Why do we use statistics at all if we can understand our results without them? The answer to this question is pretty simple. The inferential statistics let us know whether our findings are reliable, so our statistics ultimately help us determine what our findings mean. Although we can present our results in words alone, we would not know what to conclude if we did not use statistics as a tool.

In the end, our statistical tool is an implement that helps us construct something, namely, our conclusion. If we didn't have the tool, we couldn't do the construction. But once we have made what we intended, the tool recedes into the background. This is not a perfect metaphor for presenting results with statistic as a tool, but it gives the essence of the point.

The logic of statistical tests is that, for the sake of argument, researchers start with the assumption that there is no difference between an experimental and a control group. We know that in the real world, two groups may differ because of an experimental treatment but also because of other, unknown factors. The trick is to figure out if the difference is due to the experimental manipulation or to those other factors.

In using the statistical tests, we calculate how likely it would be to get differences of the size we obtained if the difference between groups was not actually due to treatments. If our difference is larger than we could reasonably expect if the treatment was ineffective, our best conclusion is that the treatment actually was effective.

The logic is similar with correlational analyses. We start by assuming that there is no relation between variables, knowing that our data will lead to a value of the correlation that differs from zero due to measurement error or factors that we don't know about. Then we compute how likely we would be to arrive at a correlation of the size we did if there were really no real relation among the variables of interest to us. If the value of the correlation coefficient is larger than would be likely if there is no relation between the variables, our best conclusion is that there must actually be a relation between the variables.

The statistics tell us whether our research results occurred because of the variables of interest to us rather than because of measurement error or factors of which we are unaware. When we describe our results, we could get away with saying what we found without mentioning those statistics. In fact, in news reports in the popular media, that is exactly what reporters do. Popular accounts of research describe what the investigators have found, but they don't give the technical details. In a formal research report, readers expect the statistical detail, although it is your job as a writer to make the point clear without confusing the issue with a mystifying statistical presentation.

The paragraphs below give the final form of our brief presentation of the results of the study on jokes and personality (Dietz et al., 2011). You have seen the verbal report in the initial presentation. It hasn't changed. Then we added the descriptive statistics; those haven't changed, either. After that, we added the figure, which (again) hasn't changed. Finally, we are adding the results of the inferential statistic, which in this situation is the analysis of variance (the *F* test). The material in italics relates to the inferential statistics.

First, we discovered that overall, level of neuroticism was not related to joke ratings. That is, participants scoring low, medium, and high on the neuroticism scale assigned the same overall ratings to jokes on a scale of 1 (*not funny*) to 7 (*very funny*). The means were 4.0, 3.9, and 3.9 for low, medium, and high neuroticism participants. *These differences were not significant, $F(2, 106) = 0.026$, $p = .974$, $\eta^2 = .048$.* Second, there was a tendency for participants to prefer sex-related jokes, followed by neutral jokes, then death-related jokes. The means were 4.2, 4.0, and 3.7, respectively. *These differences were not significant by traditional standards, but are nonetheless potentially interesting and merit further investigation, $F(2,106) = 2.680$, $p = .073$, $\eta^2 = .048$. In a factorial design, this represents a small effect (Cohen, 1988).*

However, the most interesting pattern was reflected in the *significant* interaction between the two variables, $F(4, 106) = 2.526$, $p = .045$, $\eta^2 = .087$, *which reflects a medium effect size (Cohen, 1988).* Low-neuroticism participants produced lower ratings of enjoyment for death-themed jokes and highest ratings for neutral jokes. On the other hand, the pattern for high-neuroticism participants differed. This group showed more enjoyment of sex- and death-themed jokes and least enjoyment of neutral jokes. Participants in the medium-neuroticism group tended to split the difference between the two extreme groups. *Figure 5.1 shows the relation between joke type and level of participant neuroticism.*

As you have seen in the various iterations of the presentation of results, if you start with a simple description of your results, you can communicate the important ideas simply in words. Once you have established your main point clearly, it will then be easy to add the statistical information to complete the picture. In writing an APA-style report, you will be expected to present the technical details of your statistics, but your report should be comprehensible and nearly complete without the statistics.

Deciding Whether the Results Supported Your Hypothesis

When you composed your introduction section, you expressed your expectations about how your research participants would respond. When you analyze your results, you can decide whether your participants acted as you thought they would.

When you present each of your results, you should state whether they supported your hypothesis. If your study is one in a series in which you have had success in making predictions about the outcome of earlier studies, your predictions here may have been good ones. But in some situations, especially those involving a new line of research about which we do not know very much, your hypotheses may not be supported. There is nothing wrong with this; it simply means that you have the opportunity to revise and correct your ideas. You may even be able to plan more research to help you understand why your results occurred the way they did.

It is not unusual to find that some hypotheses in a paper receive support, some do not, and some get partial support. Behavior is hard to predict because of the myriad factors involved in producing it.

Results Versus Interpretations

The results section of your paper is a description of your results. That sounds pretty obvious, but it is important to remember. In an APA-style paper, you don't present interpretations of your results with the results. You simply report the results. As a rule, there is little controversy over statements in a results section because your message is merely to say, "This is what happened."

The next step in the research process is to arrive at conclusions, to interpret your data, and to tell what they mean. As a rule, your interpretations do not belong in the results section. Rather, you present them in the discussion section, the final content-based section of your paper. In some papers, the results and discussion may be combined. For instance, if you are reporting multiple studies in a paper, you might connect the results and discussion for each study individually. If that is the case, you integrate and speculate in a final section that is often labeled *General Discussion*.

The important point is that you should make clear the distinction between what happened and what it means. For many sets of results, there is one fairly straightforward pattern of results but multiple possible interpretations. Your discussion section is where you speculate on what the results signify; it is also where a reader might come up with a different conclusion. The discussion is the focus of the next chapter.

Chapter 6

Drawing Conclusions

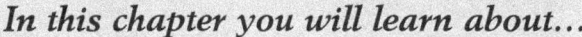

In this chapter you will learn about...

◆ Generating an Overall Statement About Support for Your Hypotheses

◆ Showing How Your Results Relate to Previous Research

◆ Conclusions and Speculation

◆ Using Results to Plan Future Research

◆ Using the Limitations in Previous Research to Move Ahead

After you analyze and describe your data, you are ready to begin dealing with the real purpose of your research, which is to answer some question about thought or behavior. Your discussion section is the place where you talk about what your results mean. As you read in the previous chapter, the results section simply describes what happened. In your discussion, you connect your research with the studies you relied on in planning your study and speculate about what mental processes are taking place in your participants.

The purposes of the discussion section of a research report are to explain the degree to which your data supported your hypotheses and to generate conclusions that go beyond your sample and your specific methodology. People are not going to be particularly impressed if your results pertain only to your sample; instead, readers want to know the general implications of your results that pertain to groups beyond your sample. Even though your perspective here will extend beyond the confines of your particular study, you should avoid overstating the importance of your results and conclusions.

Important aspects of your discussion should include statements about whether your results generalize to other populations, the importance of your specific materials and procedures and how they led to the results you obtained, and what might happen if one were to change the methodology. You should also provide the logic that has led to your conclusions. The discussion should not simply be a reiteration of the results; you should strive to present information that adds to the understanding of the topic you have studied.

Generating an Overall Statement About Support for Your Hypotheses

It's a good idea to begin your discussion with a statement about your hypotheses and whether your results support them. If your methodology is complicated or if your results have many components, the reader may not remember some of the specific points you raised in the introduction and results sections, so you will be doing your reader a favor if you indicate not only whether your results supported your hypotheses but also what aspects of your data related to the hypotheses. You should be relatively specific because if you had more than one or two hypotheses, the reader will need to be reminded about the hypothesis you are discussing.

In discussing your hypotheses, you don't need to repeat your statistics. If the reader wants the detail about means, tests of significance, effect sizes, and so forth, the reader can go back to the results section. In your discussion, you should only present the general aspects of your results that pertain to your hypotheses.

For example, Galloway and Chirico (2008) investigated whether people high in neuroticism have different humor preferences than people low in neuroticism. The researchers hypothesized that because people high in neuroticism do not respond well to novelty or to uncertain situations, such people would not enjoy nonsense humor that involved incongruities that are not resolved, that is, ideas that don't follow from one another. In other types of humor, the incongruities are successfully resolved. One of their nonsense jokes was *If it weren't for electricity, we'd all be watching television by candlelight* (p. 132).

Galloway and Chirico (2008) found that people high in neuroticism rated nonsense jokes as less funny than other types of humor. To start their discussion, they wrote the following:

The present results indicate that, as predicted, Neuroticism is related to humor structure preferences. Increases in levels of Neuroticism are associated with increased preference for incongruity-resolution compared to nonsense humor. Such a pattern is consistent with the general observation that more anxious people prefer structured situations (represented in the present research by incongruity-resolution humor) compared to unstructured situations (nonsense humor in this study). (pp. 137–138)

These investigators proposed their hypothesis in the introduction section of their research report, and then they revisited it in the discussion section. You can see that they restated their prediction (i.e., their hypotheses), gave a very general summary of their results, and connected the two.

Showing How Your Results Relate to Previous Research

Each aspect of your research so far has been important for different reasons. In the introductory phase of your project, you identified the question you wanted to answer and saw how other researchers had approached the issue. That knowledge allowed you to get a sense of the methodologies that others had used to explore a related research question. As such, you might have been able to make preliminary decisions about what materials and other stimuli would be appropriate for the study you were planning.

As you saw in earlier chapters, there are multiple ways to operationalize any given variable. For instance, if you were interested in studying the degree to which people are extraverted, friendly, or gregarious, you would have your choice of many different inventories. The website of the Oregon Research Institute's International Personality Item Pool offers five different inventories for measuring gregariousness, six for measuring friendliness, and four for extraversion. Three of these inventories appear in Table 6.1.

As you can see, the questions on the inventories have a similar focus, but the specific nature of the questions differs somewhat. The differences will have an impact on the types of conclusions you could draw. In the examples in the table, you can see that extraversion might be associated with being outgoing in a general sense, whereas the friendliness scale is more specifically focused on relating to people, and the gregariousness scale is oriented toward how a person acts in specific situations.

When you write your discussion, you should refer back to the research and theory that you relied on to produce your study to begin with. That is, if you cited research that focused on friendliness, you would likely want to talk about a person's way of interacting with others, whereas if you dealt

Table 6.1   Examples of Different Inventories that Measure a Person's Orientation to Others or to Groups, Taken From the International Personality Item Pool of the Oregon Research Institute.

Extraversion	Friendliness	Gregariousness
Feel comfortable around people	Make friends easily	Am the life of the party
Make friends easily	Am open about my feelings	Love large parties
		Joke around a lot
Am skilled in handling social situations	Act comfortably with others	Enjoy being part of a loud crowd
Am the life of the party	Radiate joy	Amuse my friends
Know how to captivate people	Warm up quickly to others	Act wild and crazy
*Have little to say	*Am hard to get to know	*Seldom joke around
*Keep in the background	*Am a very private person	*Don't like crowded events
*Would describe my experiences as somewhat dull	*Avoid contacts with others	*Am the last to laugh at a joke
*Don't like to draw attention to myself	*Keep others at a distance	*Dislike loud music
*Don't talk a lot	*Reveal little about myself	

*Reversed scored item

Source: International Personality Item Pool. From the Oregon Research Institute.

with gregariousness, you would discuss the person's orientation toward social situations. The questions on the inventories for those traits have a slightly different focus, and your conclusions should follow from the type of measurements you have made.

In addition, you should identify how your results relate to other research that you cited. In the study by Galloway and Chirico (2008), after they noted that the data supported their hypothesis, they noted how their findings fit in within the larger realm of the psychology of humor, citing others who have studied the relation between personality and humor (e.g., Hehl & Ruch, 1985). The investigators then connected other ideas involving personality characteristics. They cited Berlyne (1971) who discussed the level of arousal in people scoring high in neuroticism and related that to the fact that such people have high arousal levels so that when they encounter nonsense jokes, their arousal level increases, leading to a state of higher anxiety.

If your data do not support your hypotheses, you should try to develop explanations as to why this failure occurred. If you produced logical arguments as to why your hypotheses were reasonable, you should try to explain why your logic was problematic. Your explanations will be post hoc, that is, based on what you found, not what you expected. Theories are strongest when we can make predictions in advance that turn out to be right, but post hoc explanations can lead to more research to test the adequacy of theory and of the post hoc explanation.

Another important aspect of your discussion is to describe how your results compared to the results of other researchers. It is often difficult to figure out why other researchers' outcomes differed from yours. It could be that your methodology differed from theirs and that small differences in the method affected the outcome; it could be that for no apparent reason, either you or the other researchers were victimized by a Type I error (i.e., erroneously concluding that there was a real effect); it could be that the effect is a small one that is only apparent in certain circumstances. You don't really know which explanation is correct. But you should work to figure it out.

Trying to replicate earlier research is useful in helping us understand the validity of our studies, so if your results differ from earlier research, that might ultimately contribute to our knowledge base because your results might be more accurate than some published studies. In fact, the psychologist Brian Nosek of the University of Virginia is hoping to see how much of the psychological literature is reliable. He intends to carry out replications of all the studies that appeared in 2008 in three psychology journals, *Psychological Science*, *Journal of Personality and Social Psychology*, and *Journal of Experimental Psychology: Learning, Memory, and Cognition*. This would be a massive undertaking but could be instructive for psychology.

Some well known research that has not withstood replications include the work by Daryl Bem (2011), who reported the existence of *precognition* (conscious cognitive awareness) and *premonition* (affective apprehension) of future events; Ritchie, Wiseman, and French (2012) reported no evidence of such paranormal phenomena (and had a lot of trouble finding a journal that would publish their replication). In addition, the so-called Mozart effect (Rauscher & Shaw, 1998; Rauscher, Shaw, & Ky, 1993), wherein listening to music by Mozart supposedly enhanced spatial cognition, has failed to replicate (e.g., Steele, Bass, & Crook, 1999).

The issue of replication is important in disciplines other than psychology. For example, a researcher attempted to replicate 53 landmark studies of cancer research; only six of the replications led to the same outcome (Bartlett, 2012). And Ioannidis (2005) has demonstrated that a large proportion of published medical studies contain false (i.e., nonreplicable) outcomes.

In the end, one of the important points to recognize is that any single study may lead to erroneous conclusions. What we need to do is to make sure we keep testing psychological phenomena not only to discover whether they are real but also to help extend the knowledge base. So it is important to tie your results to those of others, regardless of whether your outcome resembles theirs.

Conclusions and Speculation

Part of your job in the discussion is to convince your reader that you have come up with a good explanation of why the results occurred the way they did. Part of your argument involves the relation between your results and those of earlier investigators, which you read about in the previous section of this chapter.

In addition, you should try to describe the mental processes that occurred while your participants went through your study. Consider the example of the research on terror management theory by Dietz, Albowicz, and Beins (2011). This research was based on that of Goldenberg, Pyszczynski, McCoy, Greenberg, and Solomon (1999) who used the following logic in their research. High levels of neuroticism are associated with difficulty in finding meaning in life, leading to high levels of anxiety. According to terror management theory, if highly neurotic people are made aware of their animal nature (i.e., humans are animals), it can increase anxiety and lead to thoughts of death because animals eventually die.

Goldenberg et al. (1999) reported that highly neurotic people who were exposed to physical aspects of sex (which they would associate with their eventual death) completed more word fragments with death-related words than did participants low in neuroticism.

My students and I wondered if exposure to sex-themed jokes would lead to thoughts of death. Our high-neuroticism participants did produce more death-related words when completing word fragments compared to low-neuroticism participants. This is a statement of the results. What is more interesting, however, is why they did this.

We concluded that jokes about sex are trigger thoughts of death in high-neuroticism participants. Why would this type of joke have such an effect? Our speculation was that because most jokes about sex are oriented toward the physical, our participants were made aware of their mortality when they read the jokes. This is a fairly straightforward interpretation that follows from the work of Goldenberg et al. (1999).

However, we went beyond this conclusion to discuss the potential role of humor in the lives of people high or low in neuroticism. That is, a good sense of humor is considered a very positive characteristic in a person, so you would imagine that jokes help foster social bonding and a consequent positive feeling. But if people respond to various types of humor somewhat negatively, it might not promote social bonding or positive reactions.

So it is possible that highly neurotic people do not regard humor as the social lubricant that people low in neuroticism do. This speculation suggests that people high in neuroticism may avoid humor or humorous situations, particularly if the themes involve sex. As you have already seen, the research on nonsense humor by Galloway and Chirico (2008) revealed that people high in neuroticism don't particularly like nonsense humor.

These studies suggest that humor takes on a different aspect for people who are high in neuroticism than it does for others. This finding could lead to more research on the topic of personality and humor. If you can speculate about why some people are made uncomfortable about humor, you can develop new research ideas. For example, in what circumstances do such people enjoy humor more or less? Can you alter their viewpoints with an experimental manipulation?

It is helpful to try and put yourself in the place of your participants. Imagine that you are going through the research process that you had set up. You may be able to get some insight into why your participants responded as they did. By doing so, you might then be able to imagine a new experiment to see if your insights are right. At this point, you can find other studies that relate to these issues so you can get an overview of our state of knowledge in this area. Others may have addressed issues similar to your proposed idea from which you can take cues.

Using Results to Plan Future Research

When you present your results, you are describing what happened. The description is not the same as what the results mean. For example, a group of psychologists studied the effect of the color of uniforms on penalties assessed against the teams. They discovered that in hockey, teams that wore black uniforms were assessed more penalties than teams that wore other colors (Webster, Urland, & Correll, 2012).

The next question is why. Certainly, the pattern of results is fascinating, but it would be interesting to know why black uniforms were associated with penalties. The researchers wondered if part of the issue was whether the home team or visiting team was more affected. They analyzed more data and ruled out that possibility. Or perhaps when people wear black uniforms, they play more aggressively, leading to more penalties. Again, further research suggested that this explanation was not the best one.

It is also possible that hockey players might be more visible to referees because of their dark uniforms. However, the researchers noted that players wearing other dark colors were not penalized as much, even though they were just as visible to referees.

One possibility that remained was that, in United States culture, black is associated with negativity. Some of this may be associated with subtle racism. The researchers don't know for sure if this is the best explanation of the results, but it presents a testable hypothesis. For example, if black is associated with negative responses in and of itself, you could present pictures of people dressed in black or other colors and ask people to rate the intelligence, personality, friendliness, and so forth. If black has a negative connotation, people wearing it might be rated less positively than are people wearing other colors.

Most research raises as many questions as it answers. After the research on uniform color, we know about the pattern of penalties in professional hockey, but we still don't know if it holds true (a) for other sports, (b) for amateur athletics, or (c) for people in black clothing in nonsporting contexts. Thus, this one study has implications to be tested in at least three follow-up studies.

When thinking about follow-up studies, it is important to keep in mind that most research involves small extensions from earlier research. So plans for new research generally have a lot in common with the previous studies. Even if your idea is not revolutionary (and just about all research is not), keep in mind that it can still move us into new territory.

Using the Limitations in Previous Research to Move Ahead

No study is perfect and provides the final answer to questions about behavior. That is simply a fact of life. You are constrained by time and other resources as to what you can do. When you develop your stimuli, you have to make choices that include some materials and omit other potentially important material. Your participants might be students from introductory psychology classes, a fairly restricted sample of the human race. There is an unlimited number of reasons for why your study leaves questions unanswered.

Such limitations are not fatal flaws in your study most of the time. Researchers recognize that when we set up our studies, we have to make compromises in order to be able to do our study. So when you discuss your research, you should point out the limitations to your work, keeping in mind that every study has them. When you spot the limitations, it means that you can plan other research that will fill in some of the gaps.

Sometimes the limitations that are problematic can be hard to spot. For example, 40 years ago, based on several studies, Horner (1972) concluded that women showed fear of success based on a desire to maintain sex-role stereotypes. The research that she conducted involved measurement of levels of motivation to succeed based scenarios in which fictitious characters (e.g., *John* and *Anne*) engaged in various behaviors. Analysis of the data revealed negative motivation to succeed by female participants.

It took 20 years before anybody spotted a particularly significant flaw in the design of the research. Ultimately, Kasof (1993) recognized a problem in the naming of the fictitious characters in research on fear of success. This type of research typically makes use of pairings like *John* and *Anne*. It turned out that the female names tended to be associated with more negative characteristics than male names were. Female names were associated with lower levels of intelligence, less positive personality characteristics, and being old fashioned.[1]

As Kasof (1993) pointed out, when the confounding effect of differences in names was removed, the supposed fear of success that women displayed tended to disappear. Researchers have not stopped investigating fear of success, though. For example, Elliot and Thrash (2004) investigated the passing on of fear of success across generations within a family.

The focus has changed from gender-related effects to a wider focus on self-handicapping as a personality trait. For instance, Uysal and Knee (2012) reported that self-control predicts self-handicapping. In a not-too-surprising discrepancy from Horner's (1972) results, Uysal and Knee also reported that "gender did not significantly correlate with any of the variables" (p. 65).

Although it took 2 decades for psychologists to recognize the limitations in the original fear of success research, an important implication for your research now is that sometimes it makes sense to replicate research with different materials. Whether you use the same materials as in earlier studies or develop new materials, you need to rely on your best judgment, in consultation with others who are familiar with the topic. Sometimes it can be a very good idea to make changes in materials when you develop research to follow from previous ideas, although you should have a reason for doing so.

---

[1]Interestingly, when Horner conducted her research, *Anne* was seen as less positive than *John*. However, 2 decades later, *Anne* was seen more favorably than *John* (Kasof, 1993). This change in relative negativity contains an important message: Sometimes materials from an earlier era may not be entirely appropriate for research at a later time.

Sometimes you don't need to wait 20 years to identify the limitations in a research project because authors frequently point them out for you. For example, most research relies on volunteers from psychology classes. Such samples might be perfectly appropriate for studying some topics. If you want to study how people learn, it may be the case that the processes that college students use to learn are just like those of everybody else. Maybe college students learn faster, but the underlying processes may be the same for just about everybody. So a college student sample could be just fine for answering such a question.

On the other hand, it may be a little less obvious that student samples are going to lead to results comparable to those from older samples. For example, regarding the phenomenon of inattention blindness, Seegmiller, Watson, and Strayer (2011) showed the video of people passing a basketball to one another while a person in a gorilla suit walks among them, beating its chest. Following the video, the participants are asked if they saw anything unusual. A surprisingly large number of people do not see the gorilla when they are trying to count the number of passes the people are making.

These researchers found that people with larger working memories are more likely to spot the gorilla than are people with lower capacities in their working memories. The participants in this study were students; the range of ages was 18 to 35, but it is likely that most of the participants were traditional, college-aged students. So what would happen with younger people? Would children show the same type of inattention blindness that college students do? How about older adults? Research has shown that people with Alzheimer's disease show high levels of inattention blindness, but the question is still open for adults with normal cognitive processes.

Another possibility is to see if anxiety or arousal is associated with differential levels of inattention blindness. As of early in 2012, there are no abstracts that connect *inattention blindness* with *arousal* or with *anxiety*. It would not be surprising to learn that people higher in arousal or anxiety would experience greater inattention blindness because their arousal would occupy some of their working memory. There has also been no exploration of the link between phenomena like stereotype threat and inattention blindness. You could set up a study that would increase participants' arousal level and then expose them to an inattention blindness task. Or you could see if people with pre-existing, high anxiety levels differ in the degree to which they exhibit inattention blindness. Or you could see if you could induce stereotype threat by creating a cover story that indicated that your participants belong to a group that regularly has difficulty with the task.

In fact, Seegmiller et al. (2011) have made similar suggestions: "Future studies addressing potential individual differences in susceptibility to inattentional blindness may find it useful to directly compare the predictive ability of working memory capacity with other cognitive measures (e.g., processing speed, personality profiles) within the same participants" (p. 790).

Another example of follow-up research based on limitations came from Adachi and Willoughby (2011) who studied the relation between video game competition and aggressive behavior. One of the limitations of their study was that they used only adolescents, so it might be productive to increase the age range; this limitation is quite typical of much psychological research because we use convenience samples, and students are conveniently available. But Adachi and Willoughby also noted that their study involved only short-term effects of the video games. They recommended a longer-term study to see if there are persistent effects.

Yet another illustration of limitations that can lead to further research came from terror management theory; Landau et al. (2006) studied men's attraction to women. They tested college students (again, a very restricted sample) and found that men, but not women, rated women as more attractive when the participants were made aware of their mortality. One caution that the researchers expressed was that the presence of a female experimenter may have influenced the responses of male participants. They offered explanations that led them to conclude that the female-male interaction was not problematic, but it still merits attention.

Still another case in which one study of terror management theory has generated a follow-up came from the research by Dietz et al. (2011) in which they presented sex-related jokes to participants and found that high-neurotic participants were more likely to have thoughts of death than low-neuroticism participants. After that, another follow-up study added a condition involving death-related jokes to the design because terror management theory postulates that subtle connections to death function differently than focal connections to death, so responses to the two types of jokes could differ (Beins, Doychak, Ferrante, Herschman, & Sherry, 2012).

Given that no study answers all of the questions about a topic, limitations to your conclusions are always a reality. But this is not a negative situation because recognition of the limitations sets the stage for more research that fills in the gaps in our knowledge. Many authors include statements of limitations to their research in the articles they publish, so it may be possible to develop your research as an extension to the work that others have done. One advantage to this approach is that the previous authors are likely to have developed useful materials and effective procedures that you can copy. This approach can save you a lot of time in developing your next project.

As you can see, your discussion section brings your project to a logical conclusion. At the same time, the discussion paves the way for the next step in the continually ongoing research process.

Chapter 7

Writing a Research Report in APA Style

❖

In this chapter you will learn about...

- ◆ Introduction Section
- ◆ Method Section
- ◆ Results
- ◆ Discussion
- ◆ References

A well-organized research report conveys your message to the reader clearly and unambiguously. Researchers in psychology, the social sciences, nursing, education, and other disciplines rely on APA style as a mechanism for getting their point across. Although there are many details associated with producing a manuscript in APA style, the conceptual organization of such a manuscript is fairly easy to comprehend.

This chapter will provide you with guidance about organizing an APA-style report. For specific formatting details, you can refer to APA's *Publication Manual of the American Psychological Association* (2010) or to any of a number of useful books that present a more condensed (and maybe easier to use) set of guidelines (e.g., Beins, 2012; Schwartz, Landrum, & Gurung, 2012).

APA has evolved from its initial seven-page incarnation (Instructions in Regard,1929) to a 272-page book in its most recent edition (American Psychological Association, 2010). It would be impractical to give a fine-grained presentation of the various details of APA style. Instead, this chapter will help you decide what to include in your manuscript and where to put it.

Table 7.1 outlines the main sections of an APA-style research report and highlights what each section contains. There is no strict formula for writing each section, but these guidelines will help you create a paper that conforms to the expectations of psychologists. When papers are appropriately formatted, readers know where to look to find the kind of information they seek.

In the sections that follow, I will present ideas on how you can organize your writing for maximal effectiveness. You will need to tailor your own paper to meet your needs because each piece of writing has its own set of demands. But you will see the general outline of a research report that you can adapt as you see fit.

Table 7.1   Components of an APA-Style Research Report and What Each Contains

Section of APA-Style Research Report	Questions Addressed in the Section
Title Page	Who are you? What is your institutional (or course) affiliation?
Introduction	What concepts are important in your research? Where did the ideas originate? What results do you expect?
Method	Who participated in your research? What apparatus and materials did you need to conduct your study? What did your participants actually do?
Results	What happened?
Discussion	What do your results mean with respect to psychological processes? What further research questions have emerged from your study? What are the limitations to your conclusions?
References	What were the sources of your ideas?

Source: Based on APA *Publication Manual*, 2010.

Introduction Section

You are telling a story when you introduce your reader to the major ideas of your study. People will want to read interesting stories but will not want to wade through boring ones. So in the introduction, start with engaging prose that captures your reader's interest and attention. The story you are telling isn't fiction, so you are bound by accuracy. But you can make your writing interesting nonetheless.

By the time the reader finishes going through this section, the development of your ideas should be quite clear. At the beginning, you need to identify the overall framework for your research question. The reader should get a sense of the general concepts before you tailor your writing to focus on the specifics of your project.

Establishing the Context of Your Study

You can engage your reader by framing your research in a context that the people are likely to find interesting. For example, Helzer and Dunning (2012) investigated people's ability to understand their own behavior in comparison to their ability to understand the behavior of others, that is, what do we know about the way we make our choices versus the way others make their choices.

These authors could have started their manuscript with a description of past research, which can be pretty complicated and which might require that the reader be familiar with the overall topic. Or they could have started with a presentation of important but abstract concepts regarding the way we make decisions. But that would not draw the reader into the story. Instead, they framed their ideas in a way that makes sense in dealing with ordinary, everyday behavior.

> The choices people make today are very often based on their expectations of success tomorrow. The decision to forgo the gym on a busy day is in part determined by one's prediction that one will make it up in the near future. Insuring one's house (or one's self) is a choice made with an eye toward tomorrow's risks. And, whether to propose to one's beloved is based on one's assessment of the future prospects of the relationship along many tomorrows. In important ways, leading a successful and satisfying life often entails accurately anticipating one's future. (Helzer & Dunning, 2012, p. 1)

This opening gives us a sense of the focus of the research (decision making) in a way that we can relate to our lives. As the journal article progresses, the authors present the technical information necessary to understand the research, but the initial ideas let us know where the researchers are likely to be taking us.

On the other hand, consider how you might have reacted if Helzer and Dunning had begun their manuscript with this statement (which, fortunately, they did not use):

> In 2006, Koehler and Poon investigated the extent to which people overpredict their future behaviors, such as whether they would donate blood. In addition, in 2009, Peetz and Buehler found that people underpredict other behaviors, like the amount of money they would save in the next month.

The research by those investigators is certainly relevant to the ideas that Helzer and Dunning (2012) studied, but this second way of starting the introduction won't capture interest as much as the approach that Helzer and Dunning actually used. Is a reader really going to be interested in the year in which the other researchers published their work? Most likely, the year is irrelevant to the reader's interest. So start with ideas that you think others will want to read.

Where Did the Ideas Come From?

Virtually every research project relies on the work of earlier investigators. When you develop your ideas, you should tell the reader how prior research and theory contributed to your work.

In studying why we make the choices we do, Helzer and Dunning (2012) cited over 60 prior works. The researchers cited 11 publications that dealt with the errors people show in decision making. They didn't give a lot of detail but did establish some of the general biases people show. That presentation lets the reader know that the researchers are studying something about errors in making choices, informing the reader of some of the ways that investigators have addressed this issue. Then they cited eight publications about the accuracy with which people predict the behavior of others. Helzer and Dunning also mention 19 citations that involved a comparison of our ability to predict our own choices versus our ability to predict the choices of others.

The sequence of ideas that Helzer and Dunning (2012) present establishes the framework of the research that they reported in their manuscript. They don't include a lot of detail about that prior research, but they give an overview of the focus of that research and set the stage for development of their new ideas.

Establishing Your Research Questions and Expectations

After you describe the previous research that is related to your study, you can begin presentation of your original ideas. That is, what is it about your work that will extend our knowledge beyond what others have already done?

Helzer and Dunning (2012) were quite clear and explicit in the goal of their research: "We placed self- and peer predictions under close scrutiny to see whether we can explain why peer predictions tend to exhibit significantly more accuracy" (p. 39).

These researchers then proceeded to describe three studies in detail that they conducted. They gave a thumbnail sketch of the major research questions in each of their experiments. Then they presented their expectations (i.e., their hypotheses) about the outcome of their studies:

> We anticipated, given past research, that peer predictions would prove more accurate. Self- and peer predictions would be equally correlated with actual performance, but peer predictions would more successfully avoid the overoptimism seen in self-predictions. This difference would be explained by trade-offs in the weight given to aspiration level versus past behavior. Whereas self predictions would weight aspiration information over past achievement, peer predictions would weight past achievement over information about aspiration. (p. 40)

After you have introduced your reader to the general focus of your research, provided information about what we already know about the topic, outlined your ideas, and generated your hypotheses, you have done everything you need in the introduction. At this point, the details of your project will make sense to your reader because those details are important to the research story that is beginning to take shape.

Method Section

The method section provides the reader with details of what happened as you collected your data. After reading this section, another person should be able to reproduce your study almost identically to the way you did it. Thus, the introduction states why you set up your study the way you did, and the method section says how you carried out your project.

In general, there are three to five subsections here. In each one, you give some fairly basic details. There is seldom any controversy regarding the methodology. Sometimes controversies occur, but when different researchers follow similar lines of research, they often share strategies. The biggest issue in this section is to decide how much detail to provide. You can see in Table 7.2 the kinds of details that appear in the subsections.

Participants

You have choices about what information to include. For example, if you are documenting changes between people of different ages, you might want to include the proportion of people in various age categories (e.g., 10–14 years, 15–19 years, 20–24 years, etc.). On the other hand, if you are

Table 7.2   Elements of the Method Section and What Questions They Address

Participants	How many participants were there? What are participant demographics? • Number or proportion of female and male participants • Ages of participants (mean age and standard deviation, range of ages; proportion of participants in relevant age categories) Any personal characteristics that pertain to your topic Any inducements to participate (e.g., extra credit in classes or an amount of money they received for their participation)
Apparatus	Equipment and instrumentation. (If you have unusual apparatus, you should describe it in detail, perhaps including illustrations or photographs. If your equipment is standard, you can simply give the manufacturer's name and the make and model number of the equipment.)
Materials	What stimuli did you use and where did you get them (e.g., reference citations)? • Stimulus words • Inventories • Surveys Limitations associated with materials (e.g., low reliability of inventories)
Procedure	What did participants actually do during the course of the study? In what order did participants engage in their tasks? How long did the study take?
Design	What were the independent and dependent variables? What analyses will there be?

not interested in developmental issues, this kind of breakdown is not terribly relevant, and you might be satisfied simply to give the range of ages or the mean and standard deviation of ages. You can take your cues from research articles that you read.

The important point here is to describe your participants in such a way that the reader knows who participated (in a general sense) and how their personal characteristics may relate to your findings.

For example, if you are studying attitudes about politics, it would be helpful to know about the political affiliations of your participants. Or if you are studying a sense of belongingness in the mathematics community by students, it would be important to identify characteristics related to such a feeling, such as participant gender and ethnicity, which is the approach that Good, Rattan, and Dweck (2012) used. In short, if there is information about your participants that would help you understand your results, you should include such detail in the description of your participants.

Apparatus and Materials

A large proportion of psychological studies do not involve specialized apparatus; on the other hand, virtually all studies include materials. The distinction between the two might be a little confusing. Apparatus refers to equipment or instrumentation. Materials involve stimuli, tests, inventories, surveys, and so forth. Or in more casual language, if you drop apparatus, it breaks. If you drop materials, they simply scatter on the floor.

Your research is likely to involve materials. The amount of detail you need to present will depend on the nature of your stimuli. If you are borrowing materials from prior research, you can omit a lot of details and refer the reader to the research from which you borrowed your materials. If you are using materials that are unique to your study, you should give more detail. For example, if you are studying learning and use words as stimuli, you should include the nature of the words, such as word frequency, category of words, and so forth because the particular stimuli you have used may affect the outcome of the study.

For instance, Marsh, Beaman, Hughes, and Jones (2012) studied the role of distraction on attention in a memory task. This is how they described their materials, which came from an existing source:

> The experiment was run using Superlab Pro software. Thirty words, taken from Positions 1 to 30, were chosen from each of 54 semantic categories in the Van Overschelde, Rawson, and Dunlosky (2004) category norm lists. Each participant received 54 trials comprising one list of 15 visually to-be-remembered words per trial. (p. 3)

Figure 7.1 shows how Thomas and Hasher (2012) detailed the type of stimuli they used in their memory research. As you can see, they provided specific information so the reader could understand how they developed their materials.

In some journal articles, authors combine materials and apparatus into a single section. In other cases, particularly when there are complex details involved, writers will create separate subsections. If your research involves no apparatus, you can delete the subsection. If your apparatus included only computers for presenting stimuli, you don't need a separate section for apparatus. On the other hand, if your equipment is complicated or extensive, you should provide the details necessary for your reader to understand exactly how you carried out your study.

One aspect of the materials subsection should be limitations associated with those materials. That is, if you were researching fear of success, you might consider using the Fear of Success Scale that Zuckerman and Allison (1976) developed. It is one of the most widely used measures in sport psychology (Metzler & Conroy, 2004). However, Metzler and Conroy pointed out that it has significant psychometric and theoretical shortcomings. So if you were to use it (as many others have done), you would want to make note of its liabilities.

Procedure

The procedure subsection provides a highly detailed depiction of what your research participants did. It offers a step-by-step description that a reader could use to understand and to reproduce your work. In general,

A *The Dig*	B *The Dig*
The car lottery *ride* wheel *was* getting basket *bumpy* outside now *that George* video *had left* addition *the* main *trainer* highway *to use* notion *the* dirt silence *road. He* stamp *was* out river *of* school, *assembly* not *having* lottery *to study* stamp *during the* summer *notion break.*	*The car* xxxxxxxx *ride* xxxxxxxx *was getting* xxxxxxxx *bumpy* xxxxxxxx *now that George* xxxxxxxx *had left* xxxxxxxx *the main* xxxxxxxx *highway to use* xxxxxxxx *the dirt* xxxxxxxx *road. He* xxxxxxxx *was out* xxxxxxxx *of school,* xxxxxxxx *not having* xxxxxxxx *to study* xxxxxxxx *during the summer* xxxxxxxx *break.*

Examples of the reading with distraction task, displaying a distracting story (Panel A) and a control story (Panel B).

Figure 7.1   Example of details of stimuli used in the memory study by Thomas and Hasher (2012).

Source: Thomas, R.C., & Hasher, L. (2012). Copyright © 2012 American Psychological Association. Used with permission.

the material in this section involves only those aspects of the research that involve the participants. When they arrived at the laboratory, what is the first thing they did? Then what happened? You trace their activity as they progressed through the study. If your participants completed a set of inventories, list those materials and the order in which the participants completed them.

If you are using an experimental manipulation, you should make clear your independent and dependent variables. In addition, it is important to differentiate the various conditions of groups and what participants in them went through. What did the experimental group do, and how did it differ from what the control group (or other experimental groups) did?

If your participants completed the study in a lab, you should mention whether they were tested individually or in groups. Further, today's research methodologies often include online data collection. You obviously do not know what your participants were actually doing if they completed the study somewhere else. So all you can do is to outline the way the study is set up. The reader will know that how the participant approached the task is uncertain, but the quality of data from Internet-based research seems generally comparable to that generated in laboratories (Buhrmester, Kwang, & Gosling, 2011; Gosling, Vazire, Srivastava, & John, 2004).

Design

Some authors include a mention of the design in the method section. Doing so can help the reader understand the overall structure of your research. If you explained that you created a 3 × 4 factorial design, the reader will know that you manipulated two independent variables, one with three conditions and the other with four. If there were any repeated measures, you would indicate that as well. In addition, it can be illustrative for readers if you identify specifically the conditions associated with each independent variable.

For example, a student and I exposed participants to one of five messages about jokes they would be rating. We told the participants (a) that the jokes were quite unfunny, (b) that the jokes were not very funny, (c) no information about how funny the jokes would be, (d) that the jokes were very funny, or (e) that the jokes were hysterically funny. When you describe the design of your study, the reader can see and understand the overall structure of your study.

Results

When you present your results, it is best to keep your presentation as simple as you can while getting your message across effectively. You will have to present some technical information, but try not to overwhelm your reader with excessive detail. It is important to keep in mind that if you fail to convey your message, it is not your reader's fault; it is yours. Your job is to make your reader's life as easy as possible.

In formatting the results section, unless your research design is fairly complex, you can present your results in a single, undivided section. On the other hand, if you have multiple types of measurements, it can be useful to create subsections that deal with them individually.

Authors frequently begin their presentation of the data with a statement as to whether the data support the hypotheses that appeared in the introduction section. In much research, there is likely to be partial support for hypotheses. Results are not usually as neat and clean as we would like them to be. In textbooks, results are frequently depicted as conforming perfectly with hypotheses or as definitely refuting hypotheses, but in most research projects, the truth is somewhere in between. You should not try to hide the fact that your hypotheses were not uniformly supported.

After dealing with your hypotheses, it is typical to describe your results in more detail. Before you dive into your statistics, though, it is often useful to write your message using only (or mostly) words, omitting numbers. By using this approach, you are likely to be clearer in your presentation than if you used a lot of numbers at the start. Using words forces you to focus on the concepts, which are most important, rather than the numbers, which are less important.

In everyday life, we talk to people using words, not numbers, when we want to explain something. In your results, if you start with words, you may be better able to produce a comprehensible statement of the results. You can later add the numerical information to support your words. Words will be better for introducing your reader to the concepts you want to advance. The numbers can wait.

Common elements in the results include descriptive statistics like the group means and standard deviations. If you are comparing groups, after you say that the experimental group had a higher mean than the control group, you can add further supporting detail, like the results of statistical tests that indicate whether any effects are statistically significant.

Thus, the order of writing your results might be a verbal description of the results, presentation of descriptive statistics, and then statements of statistical significance. The first, and most important in terms of conveying your message, are the words. We use the statistics as tools to help make our argument, but the verbal argument contains the important concepts.

If you have multiple variables in your research design, you may want to use either a table or a figure to present your results. These two elements allow the reader to get an overall picture of your results at a single glance. In addition, if you have a large number of groups, it can be difficult to make sense of a long string of numbers embedded in the text.

Another approach to presenting results is to make your ideas as concrete as possible. That is, you may want to make frequent use of *that is* kinds of statements. Such statements can put your results into context for the reader. It is sometimes tempting to make a single lengthy list of means across groups because it is clear to you what you mean. But you know your topic much better than your reader will, so you should expand on your verbal statements and use figures and tables to fill in any gaps in your reader's understanding.

Figure 7.2 provides an example of how to present the results of multiple groups. The concise presentation of group means in the graph and the figure caption provide the necessary detail. This kind of graph allows the reader to take in a lot of information at once, seeing the relation among groups. Consider the ease of attending to the overall pattern of results in the graph compared to this following verbal presentation that (thankfully) the authors did not use and that you would not want to emulate:

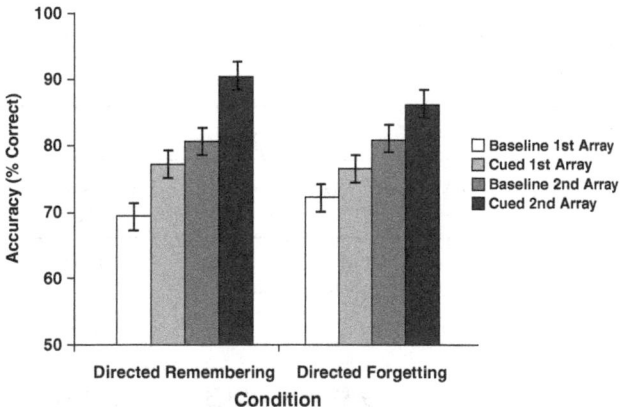

Mean accuracy (percentage correct) as a function of experimental Condition, cue presentation, and array presentation order. The left two bars in each condition represent performance when the first array was tested. The right two bars in each conditin represent performance when the second array was tested. Error bars show the 95% within-subject confidence intervals (Loftus & Loftus, 1988).

Figure 7.2   Example of formatting of figure showing values for eight different experimental conditions. Listing the values of the eight conditions in the text would make it hard for a reader to put it all together.

Source: Williams, M., & Woodman, G. F. Copyright © 2012 American Psychological Association.

In the directed remembering condition, the mean for the baseline first array was 69; for the cued first array, 77; for the baseline second array, 81; and for the cued second array, 91. In the directed forgetting condition, the mean for the baseline first array was 74; for the cued first array, 76; for the baseline second array, 82; and for the cued second array, 86.

I hope you can see why you would not want to present the means for these eight groups in the text itself. It is very difficult to make any comparisons across groups. One point to remember, though, is that graphs do not always allow you to identify the exact values depicted in the figure. So the means given above are only approximate. This is one drawback of figures: They do not generally present exact values. If you want to give exact values, you can put them in a table. Figure 7.3 is an APA-formatted table that shows how you could create a table with these values.

Incidentally, if you present data in a figure or a table, you don't repeat it in the text. Instead refer in the text to the figure or table so the reader knows when it relates to the text.

Table 1

Mean Accuracy as a Function of Experimental Condition, Cue Presentation, and Array Presentation Order.

Task	Condition				
	Baseline first array	Cued first array	Baseline second array	Cued second array	
Directed remembering	69.0	77.0	81.0	91.0	(79.5)
Directed forgetting	74.0	76.0	82.0	86.0	(79.5)
	(71.5)	(79.5)	(81.5)	(88.5)	

Figure 7.3   APA format of a table with multiple means. The values in parentheses, the marginal means, represent the mean for all groups in a given condition. The mean values listed are approximations taken from the journal article by Williams and Woodman (2012), who presented the results in a figure, so only approximate values are possible.

Source: Based on data from Williams, M., & Woodman, G. F. Copyright © 2012 American Psychological Association. Used with permission.

Finally, when you present inferential statistics, you are telling readers whether your results are significant, that is, reliable. You can see the formats for presenting the common inferential statistics in Table 7.3. If your use different statistical tests, you can refer to the formatting in the APA publication manual (American Psychological Association, 2010) or any of the various books devoted to APA style (e.g., Beins, 2012; Schwartz et al., 2012).

Table 7.3   Format of Common Statistical Tests and When You Use Them

Use of the Statistic	What Statistic to Use	Example of Format
Comparison of two means	t test	$t(212) = 1.58, p = .115$
Comparison of two or more means	Analysis of variance	$F(2, 344) = 3.272, p = .039$
Find relation between two variables	Correlation coefficient	$r(216) = .383, p < .001$

Note: If the probability level is .000 when carried out to three decimal places, indicate significance as $p < .001$. Otherwise, use the exact probability value.

Discussion

You are nearing the end of your project now. You have identified your research question and its rationale, what tools you used to address your question, and the outcome of your data collection. Now you talk about what it all means.

Your discussion section begins with an overall statement of the results. You don't repeat what you just said in the results section. Rather, you give an overview of the outcome. Readers who want specific details can refer back to the results section.

As an example, consider the research by Witt and Brockmole (2012) on how people who are holding guns perceive the world around them. In short, with five experiments, the researchers demonstrated that if a person is holding a gun (a Nintendo Wii Magnum Gun), the person is more likely to judge ambiguous objects held by others as guns compared to when the person is holding a neutral object (e.g., a shoe or a foam ball).

The researchers presented their results in detail for the five studies, and then began their discussion in a way that put the important issues in context. They focused on the concepts rather than the specific data:

The familiar saying goes that when you hold a hammer, everything looks like a nail. The apparent harmlessness of this expression fades when one considers what happens when a person holds a gun. We have shown here that, having the opportunity to use a gun, a perceiver is more likely to classify objects held by others as guns and, as a result, to engage in threat-induced behavior (in this case, raising a firearm to shoot). (Witt & Brockmole, 2012, p. 7)

Their opening is a succinct, engaging way to begin their discussion of how what people are holding affects what they see and the judgments they make. As the researchers later pointed out, these results have implications not only for theoretical studies of object perception but also for public safety. Consider, for example, localities in which carrying a gun is legal (and maybe even encouraged). Are people in that place more likely to interpret ambiguous objects as guns and, consequently, to shoot their own guns? According to the authors, about 25% of police shootings are of unarmed people, perhaps because of the dynamics that the researchers are studying.

One purpose of the discussion is to interpret why behaviors occur as they do, so Witt and Brockmole (2012) speculated that the increased likelihood of perceiving guns in the environment and to move to shoot is due to so-called event coding. That is, they reasoned that when a person plans to use an object (e.g., a gun), it biases the individual to perceive guns. They also noted that when the object was a shoe, participants tended to perceive ambiguous objects as shoes, so the researchers' interpretation is not limited to firearms. Witt and Brockmole explained their results in terms of cognitive processes on the part of participants.

Sometimes, however, when you do research, you do not end up with statistically significant results. When that occurs, you try to explain why you failed to get the effects you anticipated. It is often difficult to do so because there are many possible reasons for nonsignificant effects, including the actual absence of an effect or measurement error or inappropriate stimuli or inattention or fatigue on the part of the participants and so forth. In contrast, it is generally the case that significant effects are likely to be caused by fewer potential factors, the most likely (we hope) our experimental manipulations.

Another difficulty in interpreting results occurs when you fail to reproduce results that others have gotten. The reason for the inconsistency could be due to problems in your research, but it could also be due to problems in the other research. Those investigators might have experienced a Type I error, achieving statistical significance when there really isn't an effect. The problem is that you don't know. You seldom see investigators trying to explain away nonsignificant results in a journal article because, as researchers know, it is hard to get a journal to publish an article that does not have statistically significant outcomes. But if you have finished a project that resulted in nonsignificant results, you should try to figure out what might have led to unexpectedly nonsignificant (and maybe disappointing) results.

After explaining your results, significant or not, you can pose possibilities for further research on the topic in order to fill in gaps in our knowledge of the area. For instance, Uysal and Knee (2012) investigated the relation between self-handicapping (i.e., purposefully sabotaging the likelihood of success in a future task) and self-control; they found that low self-control predicts self-handicapping behavior.

Based on their results, on other research, and on theory, these researchers drew the conclusion that it is the self-control factor that exerts a causal effect on self-handicapping. They then identified further research projects that follow from their work. For example, they suggested that people can actively learn the strategy of self-handicapping based on their behavior and experience; this idea has potential for a longitudinal research project. They also wondered whether self-handicapping might relate to impression management, also a testable hypothesis.

It is virtually always the case that a good research project will open doors to subsequent work. You manage to answer some questions, but there are always gaps. For example, Dietz, Albowicz, and Beins (2011) reported that jokes with sexual themes led to thoughts of death among people scoring high in neuroticism. A new question, which Beins, Doychak, Ferrante, Herschman, and Sherry (2012) investigated, was whether exposure to death-themed jokes would have the same effect. So they created a set of jokes that were either sex themed, death themed, or neutral. It turned out that sex and death led to the same pattern of results, which differed from the results of exposure to neutral jokes.

Finally, after researchers discuss the reasons for their results, they commonly note the limitations of their study. In the case of Uysal and Knee's (2012) study on self-handicapping, they noted two limitations in their work. The first was that they used a correlational design, so they could not assess whether low self-control might have caused self-handicapping or the other way around. They recommended a study that would manipulate the state of a participant's self-control (as opposed to the trait) to see if changes in level of self-control led to changes in self-handicapping. A second limitation was that their samples consisted mostly of women, so the generalizability of their finding to men is not known. That limitation, too, could be remedied with future research.

References

When you have finished explaining your results, identifying potential follow-up studies, and noting the limitations of your research, you are nearly finished with your project. The only section of the paper that remains is the reference section.

In scientific research, the references are not the same as a bibliography. In your research report, you include in the references section only those citations that you actually *referred* to in your writing. If you didn't mention a reference in your paper, you don't include it in your reference section.

There are varied kinds of sources that you might cite, but journal articles, books, and book chapters are the three main kinds. An example of each appears in Table 7.4. You can find more unusual references in the APA publication manual or in the various books devoted to APA style (e.g., Beins, 2012; Schwartz et al., 2012).

Table 7.4

Reference Formats for Journal Articles, Books, and Book Chapters in APA Style.

Journal article	Buhrmester, M., Kwang, T., & Gosling, S. D. (2011). Amazon's Mechanical Turk: A new source of inexpensive, yet high-quality, data? *Perspectives on Psychological Science, 6,* 3–5. Note: Do not include the issue number for most scientific journals; the volume number will suffice.
Journal article with more than seven authors	Löckenhoff, C. E., De Fruyt, F., Terracciano, A., McCrae, R. R., De Bolle, M., Costa, P. R., . . . Yik, M. (2009). Perceptions of aging across 26 cultures and their culture-level associates. *Psychology and Aging, 24,* 941–954. doi:10.1037/a0016901 Note: Include only first six authors listed, followed by three ellipsis points, and the very last author of the paper.
Book	Beins, B. C. (2012). *APA style simplified: Writing in psychology, education, nursing, and sociology.* Malden, MA: Wiley-Blackwell.
Chapter in a book	Beins, B. C. (2012). Jean Piaget: Theorist of the child's mind. In W. Pickren, D. A. Dewsbury, & M. Wertheimer (Eds.). *Portraits of pioneers in developmental psychology* (pp. 89–107). London, England: Taylor & Francis.

Appendix A

Creating a Poster Presentation

❖

You can use Microsoft PowerPoint or other presentation software to create a poster for displaying your research at a conference. The mechanics of designing the poster are fairly straightforward. As always, however, the most challenging part is deciding what to include in your poster. You will have too much information to include it all, so you have to make choices.

If you have written an APA-style research report, you can use your paper as a guide regarding what to put on the poster, but a significant task will be to strike a balance in terms of the amount of material you include. You want to present enough information to give the viewer a good sense of what you did, why and how you did it, what the results were, and what you concluded, but you don't want to pack so much information on the poster that nobody will want to read it. If there is too much text and if it is too small to read easily, people are likely to walk by your poster without giving it much attention because going over it would involve too much work.

Setting Up the PowerPoint File

The first step in setting up the PowerPoint file is to tell PowerPoint (the steps outlined here are for PowerPoint 2007, currently the most widely used version) what size you want your poster to be. To do this, you will not use any of the standard slide sizes. Instead, you will select a customized size to match your needs. It is common at conferences that you will be allotted a maximum size for your poster. A display size of 3 × 4 feet is not unusual. Table A.1 indicates the steps for creating the poster.

Table A.1   Steps for Setting Up a PowerPoint Poster

The Step	What the Step Does
Select **Design** on the Quick Access Toolbar at the top of the page. Go to *Page Setup* and select *Slides sized for Custom.*	Allows you to select the dimensions of the poster
For **Width**, enter the larger of the two dimensions of the poster (e.g., enter 48 inches for a 3' × 4' poster).	Sets up the longer of the two dimensions of your poster
For **Height**, enter the smaller of the two dimensions (e.g., enter 36 inches for the 3' × 4' poster).	Sets up the shorter of the two dimensions of your poster
Make sure the **Slide Orientation** is set for *Landscape.*	Orients the poster so the longer dimension of the poster is horizontal
Hit *OK.*	Sets up the slide for your material
Select **View** and enable *Ruler* and *Gridlines* by checking the appropriate boxes.	Allows you to see how the various components of your content are positioned relative to one another (Note: The gridlines appear on your computer monitor, but they will not appear on your printed poster.)
Select **Home**, and in **Layout**, select *Blank*	Sets up a completely empty slide

After you set up the slide size and orientation, it is time to add content. An easy way to do this is to create separate text boxes for each component of the poster. Select **Insert** in the Quick Access Toolbar at the top of the PowerPoint screen and then choose *Text Box.* When you click the mouse on the poster, a text box will appear.

Figure A.1 shows how you can set up your poster. Clearly, it is not the only approach, but it will give you an idea of what options are available. It is based on research that my students and I conducted and then presented at a convention of the Eastern Psychological Association (Ippolito & Beins, 2011). In this example, each heading and each section involves its own text box. Thus, the label for the abstract is a text box set up so that the background is a different color than the rest of the background, highlighting it. The abstract itself is a separate box. The same pattern holds true for each section. You may want to make visible the lines around the boxes.

Depending on how much space you have and how much information you want to present, you can adjust the size of the type in your poster.

One advantage of this approach is that you can use your mouse to drag the boxes to different parts of the poster if you want to do so. For figures, you can create picture files and import them into the poster. You can also drag them from place to place and resize them with the mouse. You can also use color to highlight important aspects of your poster.

In the end, you want a poster that contains enough substance to be interesting, but not so much material that people won't want to read it. A visual balance between text, figures or tables, and space is important.

Suggestions for Poster Content

As I noted above, you shouldn't include too much information in the poster. It is a significant abbreviation of a full research report. There are some elements that are useful to include as you reduce the level of detail you present. In many cases, you can introduce the material with extended bulleted points.

Introduction

In this part of the poster, you might be able to encapsulate the source of your ideas with two or three bulleted points describing previous research that led to your ideas. You won't be able to give a lot of the detail from the previous research, so present only the most salient ideas from the earlier studies. Unless the authors of that work are particularly important, you should not focus on names; rather, describe the concepts.

You can then list the basic research questions you addressed in your research. Figure A.1 shows how my student and I presented our research questions. There were more than two questions relevant to our research, but with the limited space in a poster, we restricted our presentation to two main questions.

Method

As you can see in the figure, we presented only a little information about the participants, the number and the gender breakdown. When you are presenting your poster, if people ask about the details, you can tell them what they want to know. Or you can have a handout with more detail, as with a full research report.

Regarding apparatus and materials, you should highlight the important elements, but you can rely on a handout to present more detailed information. In terms of the procedure, you need to give some detail about what the participants actually did, but you should keep in mind the balance between offering too much information (which people won't read) and too little information for people to understand what happened.

Sometimes you can consider a graphic display of the procedure that takes the place of paragraphs. For example, Figure A.2 shows the order of tasks for the study illustrated in Figure A.1. It is easy to see at a glance what happened and when. The drawback is that figures can take up more space than simple bulleted points. It is a choice that you can make based on your best judgment.

Results

Visual displays of your results will be helpful for viewers. So whenever you can, you should display graphs and tables that depict your results at a single glance. You will supplement the visual elements with verbal descriptions, but people attending poster sessions are likely to appreciate graphic displays because such displays give them the information they want in an easy-to-comprehend format.

In addition, as you can see in Figure A.1, you can highlight some of your text as a signal to the viewer that the material is important in understanding the data. As a rule, the more guidance you can give the viewer about where to look for the most critical information, the better your communication will be.

Discussion

Your interpretations and conclusions need to be brief in the discussion section. Because you need to restrict your presentation to the bare essentials, you will have to make decisions and compromises about what to include. It is usually the case that you could present much more in the way of speculation and interpretation than will fit in the poster.

Again it is important to remember that if you include too much information, people will not be willing to read it. With respect to the discussion, if they have read through the previous sections, they may not have the patience to wade through a complex discussion section. If you limit your presentation to two or three main points, the viewer will be more likely to attend to them.

Sense of Humor: Are We All Above Average?
Alycia Ippolito & Bernard C. Beins (Ithaca College)

Abstract

People attribute certain personality characteristics to others, depending on the perceived sense of humor of those others. In this study, we investigated whether participants would attribute the same characteristics to themselves that previous research has shown that they attribute to others. The results revealed that personality stereotypes associated with others show some similarity to self-reported traits. In addition, contrary to numerous claims, people can accurately indicate their relative level of sense of humor.

Basic Questions

1. Do people assess the relation between their personalities and humor as they assess that relation in others?[2]

2. Can people accurately report their level of sense of humor in relation to others?[1, 4-5]

Method

Participants

65 undergraduates volunteered
43 women, 22 men

Stimuli

Multidimensional Sense of Humor Scale (MDSHS)[6,7]

Neuroticism, Extraversion, Openness, Conscientiousness, and Agreeableness Scales[3]

Procedure

Participants completed the MDSHS to obtain an objective measure of sense of humor

Participants completed self-report scales to measure level of factors on the Five-Factor Model of Personality: Extraversion, Neuroticism, Agreeableness, Conscientiousness, and Openness

Testing occurred in groups or individually online

Sense of Humor Scale

Characteristics

The MDSHS revealed subcomponents of personality:

- Social uses of humor
- Production of humor
- Using humor for coping
- Negative attitude toward humor

Sense of Humor and Funniness

Participants self-rated on:

- How funny they thought they were
- Their level of sense of humor
- Do they recognize the humor in most jokes?

Results

Personality and Sense of Humor

Does low sense of humor reveal high neuroticism?

Previous research[2] identified an inverse relation between sense of humor in hypothetical others (stereotypes of others) and their neuroticism.

Our research reveals a similar, but marginal, negative relation between a person's self-reported levels of humor and level of neuroticism, $r(63) = -.208$, $p = .096$.

Do extraverted people show high levels of sense of humor?

People with high level of sense of humor show high levels of humor production, but not overall sense of humor.

This finding matches stereotypes reported in earlier research[2]. The stereotype of extraverted people who are humorous has some validity, $r(63) = .418$, $p < .001$.

Results

Do openness to experience and agreeableness relate to humor?

People with high scores on these traits show greater appreciation of humor, $r(63) = .258$, $p = .038$ and $r(63) = .391$, $p = .001$, respectively, but not production or coping. These findings replicates earlier research on stereotypes of others[2].

Do we know how funny we are?

Previous claims: people don't know their SoH[1, 5-6], but rate themselves highly.

People are reluctant to rate themselves as low in humor. But MDSHS score for humor production relates to self-reported level of funniness, $r(63) = .518$, $p < .001$, and self-reported SoH correlates with MDSHS score, $r(63) = .547$, $p < .001$.

People know their humor competence and report it veridically: Not everybody is above average

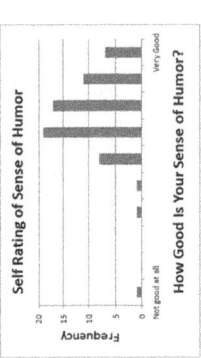

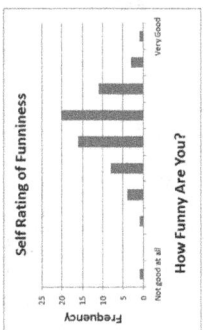

Results

Participants differentiated between how funny they are ($M = 7.7$) and what was their level of sense of humor ($M = 6.6$), $F(1, 63) = 31.295$, $p < .001$.

Conclusions

When people relate their own personality traits and sense of humor, they generate a similar pattern of results than when they rate hypothetical others, suggesting that stereotypes about personality and humor have some validity.

Some of the Big Five personality traits are reliably associated with dimensions of humor in theoretically predictable ways.

Contrary to previous reports[1, 3-4] we have seen, people can place themselves accurately on a continuum of how funny they are. Lower sense of humor is associated with lower self-ratings of humor; high sense of humor is associated with higher self ratings.

References

1. Allport, G. W. (1961). *Pattern and grown in personality.* New York: Holt, Rinehart, and Winston.
2. Cann, A., & Calhoun, L. G., (2001). Perceived personality associations with differences in sense of humor: Stereotypes of hypothetical others with high or low senses of humor. *Humor, 14,* 117-130.
3. Fine, G. A. (1975). Components of perceived sense of humor ratings of self and others. *Psychological Reports, 36,* 793-794.
4. International Personality Item Pool (2001). A scientific collaboratory for the development of advanced measures of personality traits and other individual differences. Retrieved April 17, 2006 from http://ipip.ori.org.
5. Kruger, J., & Dunning, D. (1999). Unskilled and unaware of it: How difficulties in recognizing one's own incompetence lead to inflated self-assessments. *Journal of Personality and Social Psychology, 77,* 1121-1134.
6. Lefcourt,, H. M., & Martin, R. A. (1986). *Humor and life stress. Antidote to adversity.* New York: Springer/Verlag.
7. Thorson, J. A., & Powell, F. C. (1993). Development and validation of a multidimensional sense of humor scale. *Journal of Clinical Psychology, 49,* 13-23.
8. Thorson, J. A., & Powell, F. C. (1993). Sense of humor and dimensions of personality. *Journal of Clinical Psychology, 49,* 799-809.

Source: Ippolito, A., & Beins, B. C. (2011).

References

The reference section may be the least important section of a poster. It does not really help the viewer understand your research and conclusions, so you can keep it to a minimum, particularly if you have a handout that contains more detailed information.

The poster in Figure A.1 did not use APA style for reference citations in the text. In a written research report, you would want to conform to APA style, but that kind of presentation takes up space. Thus, it may make sense to alter the nature of your citations so you don't fill precious space with less important information.

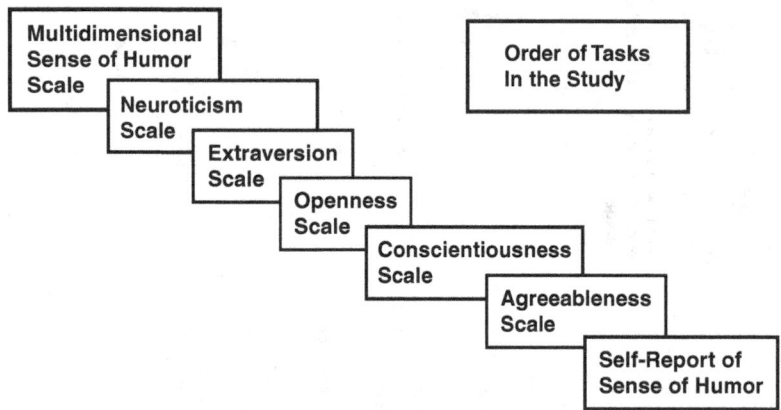

Figure 1. Order of participants' tasks. They completed the sense of Humor Scale (24 items), then the personality inventories (10 items each), ending with three self-report ratings of their sense of humor, their funniness, and their ability to recognize the humor in jokes.

Figure A.2   Illustration of how you could depict the order of completion of tasks in the study illustrated in Figure A.1.

Appendix B

Using SPSS for Data Analysis[1]

T he most widely used software for data analysis in psychology is SPSS. It is a powerful data analysis system that can generate complex output of many different statistical techniques. In this appendix, I will highlight some of the most common statistical tests that you are likely to use in your research.

Table B.1 lists the tests and the situations in which you use them. If your research involves more complex designs, you may need to refer to a manual specifically oriented toward SPSS. Steps for computing each of these statistics appear below.

Table B.1   Common Research Designs and Statistical Tests Accompanying Them

Research Design	Statistical Test
Comparison of means of two independent groups	Independent-groups *t* test (Note: You can also use a one-way ANOVA[a] here.)
Comparison of means of two related or correlated groups, including repeated measures designs	Dependent-groups *t* test (Note: You can also use a repeated measures ANOVA here.)
Comparison of means of more than two groups with a single independent variable	One-way ANOVA with post hoc comparison

(Continued)

[1]Copyright Bernard C. Beins 2012. Used with permission.

Table B.1   (Continued)

Comparison of means of groups on more than one independent variable	Univariate ANOVA (General Linear Model)
Comparison of means of more than two groups with a single independent variable that involves repeated measures	Repeated measures ANOVA (General Linear Model)
Test of whether two variables are correlated	Pearson product-moment correlation (Note: You can use the standard Pearson correlation for analyses using the phi coefficient with dichotomous data and correlations on ranked data. The result will be the same as if you used the specialized formula for phi or for correlations with ranked data. If ranks are tied, the Pearson formula will be more accurate.)
Predicting a criterion score based on one or more predictor variables.	Linear regression

[a]ANOVA = Analysis of variance.

Steps in Conducing Data Analysis in SPSS

Independent-Groups _t_ Test	
Step 1	Analyze –> Compare means –> Independent-groups t test
Step 2	Move dependent variable into the box labeled _Test variable_.
Step 3	Move independent variable into the box labeled _Grouping variable_.
Step 4	Click on _Define groups_ and enter the group numbers (e.g., 1 and 2) into the boxes. Select _Continue_.
Step 5	Select _OK_ to tell SPSS to do the computations.

In the example, my students and I computed the number of death-related words that participants generated from word fragments. For example, the fragment _COFF _ _ could be completed either as _coffee_ or _coffin_. Did participants differ in the number of death-related word fragments they generated depending on whether they were lower or higher in their neuroticism level? Terror management theory predicts that participants scoring high in neuroticism will be primed to think of death when they are reminded of the physical aspects of sex. The annotated output appears in Figure B.1.

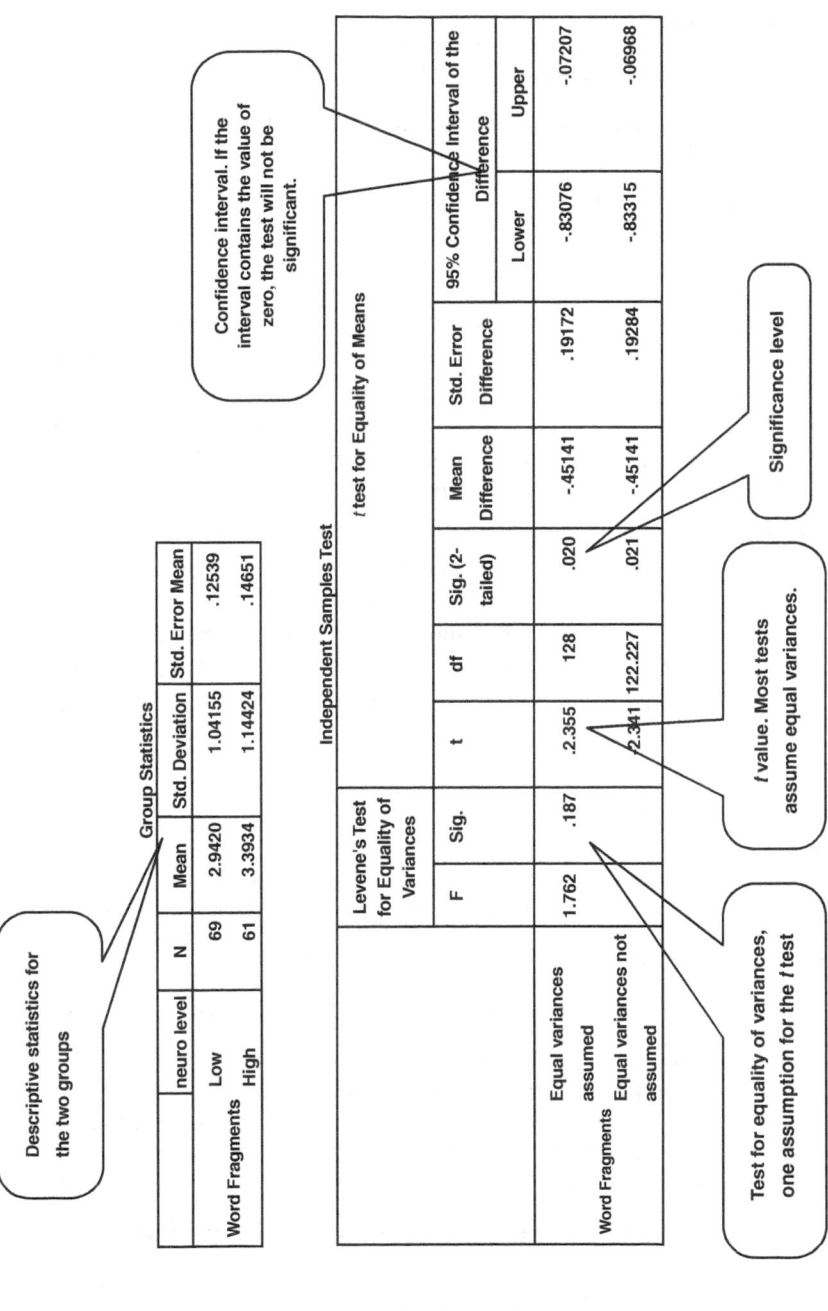

Figure B.1 Annotated SPSS output for an independent-groups *t* test. The value of *t* is not significant, as reflected in the *Sig.* value that is greater than .05 and the confidence interval, which contains the value of zero. Because the test of equality of variances is not significant, you would use the value of *t* for the *Equal variances assumed* calculation.

Dependent-Groups *t* Test

Step 1	Analyze –> Compare means –> Paired samples *t* test
Step 2	Move paired dependent variables into the box labeled *Paired variables*
Step 3	Select *OK* to tell SPSS to do the computations.

As you can see from the output, the mean number of death-related word fragments was greater for participants with higher scores on the neuroticism inventory.

Figure B.2 shows the output of a dependent-measures *t* test. In this research, we measured participants' levels of sexism toward women on a scale developed by Glick and Fiske (1999). That scale measures two constructs, benevolent sexism and hostile sexism. The question here is whether our participants are different in their measured levels of the two kinds of sexism.

As you can see in the output, the significance level is .880, reflecting a nonsignificant difference on the two measures. The confidence intervals include the value of zero, another indication that the difference was not statistically significant.

One-Way ANOVA

Step 1	Analyze –> Compare means –> One-way ANOVA
Step 2	Move dependent variable into the box labeled *Dependent List.*
Step 3	Move independent variable into the box labeled *Factor.*
Step 4	Click on *Post Hoc* (if you want to compare individual groups in addition to computing the overall *F* value) and select which post hoc test you want to use. There are several options. For this example, we will use Fisher's Least Significant Difference (LSD) test. Select *Continue.*
Step 5	Select *Options* and choose *Descriptive Statistics.* Then select *Continue.*
Step 6	Select *OK* to tell SPSS to do the computations.

Paired Samples Statistics

		Mean	N	Std. Deviation	Std. Error Mean
Pair 1	ASIB	3.4362	60	.62234	.08034
	ASIH	3.3497	60	.74700	.09644

Descriptive statistics for the paired groups

Paired Samples Correlations

		N	Correlation	Sig.
Pair 1	ASIB & ASIH	60	.394	.002

Correlation between paired scores. Normally, you do not need this information for your analysis.

Paired Samples Test

		Paired Differences					t	df	Sig. (2-tailed)
					95% Confidence Interval of the Difference				
		Mean	Std. Deviation	Std. Error Mean	Lower	Upper			
Pair 1	ASIB-ASIH	.08652	.76113	.09826	-.11011	-.28314	.880	59	.382

t value. Because the *Sig.* value is greater than .05, we do not regard it as statistically significant.

Figure B.2   Annotated SPSS output for a dependent measures (paired samples) *t* test. The significance value is .382, which is larger than the traditional value of .05, so we would not regard it as statistically significant.

In this example, we are measuring the incidence of death-related word fragment completions as a function of level of neuroticism.

The ANOVA summary table depicted in Figure B.3 indicates that there is a statistically significant effect of level of neuroticism. The post hoc analysis using the LSD test indicates that the lowest level of neuroticism is statistically different from the middle group and may differ from the highest group.

Factorial Design (More Than One IV and One DV)

Step 1	Analyze –> General Linear Model –> Univariate
Step 2	Move dependent variable (DV) into the box labeled *Dependent Variable.*
Step 3	Move independent variables (IV) into the box labeled *Fixed Factors.* (Note: Most research in psychology involves factors. Unless you have randomly selected your conditions from a larger set of conditions, you don't want to designate *Random Factors.*)
Step 4	Click on *Post Hoc* and move your independent variables into the box labeled *Post Hoc Tests.* Then select the post hoc test you want to use. We will use the LSD test.
Step 5	Click on *Options* and move the variables into the box labeled *Display Means for.*
Step 6	In *Display*, select *Estimates of Effect Size.*
Step 7	Select *OK* to tell SPSS to do the computations.

This data analysis continues the example of completion of word fragments with death-related words. The two independent variables are type of joke (death related, neutral, and sex related) and level of neuroticism (low, medium, and high). The output for this data analysis reveals statistically significant effects both for joke type and for neuroticism level. The interaction between the two variables is not significant. You can see the SPSS output in Figures B.4 and B.5.

The post hoc analysis reveals that participants rating sex-related and death-related jokes completed the word fragments with death-related words about the same, but they generated more death-related fragments than the participants rating neutral jokes. The low-neuroticism participants generated fewer death-related fragments than the middle- or high-neuroticism groups.

The significance levels for two of the comparisons were .051 and .055. If you use the traditional cutoff for significance of .05, these would not be

Descriptives

Death-related word fragments

	N	Mean	Std. Deviation	Std. Error	95% Confidence Interval for Mean		Minimum	Maximum
					Lower Bound	Upper Bound		
.00	115	2.40	1.083	.101	2.20	2.60	0	6
1.00	125	2.75	1.097	.098	2 56	2.95	0	6
2.00	107	2.69	1.201	.116	2.46	2.92	0	5
Total	347	2.62	1.133	.061	2.50	2.74	0	6

> Descriptive statistics for the three groups

ANOVA

Death-related word fragments

	Sum of Squares	df	Mean Square	F	Sig.
Between Groups	8.289	2	4.144	3.272	.039
Within Groups	435.734	344	1.267		
Total	444.023	346			

> ANOVA summary table. The *F* value is considered significant because the Sig. value is less than .05.

Post Hoc Tests

Multiple Comparisons

Death-related word fragments

LSD

(I) Neuroticism Level	(J) Neuroticism Level	Mean Difference (I-J)	Std. Error	Sig.	95% Confidence Interval	
					Lower Bound	Upper Bound
.00	1.00	-.352*	.145	.016	-.64	-.07
	2.00	-.292	.151	.055	-.59	.01
1.00	.00	.352*	.145	.016	.07	.64
	2.00	.060	.148	.684	-.23	.35
2.00	.00	.292	.151	.055	-.01	.59
	1.00	-.060	.148	.684	-.35	.23

*. The mean difference is significant at the 0.05 level.

> Significant differences are indicated with asterisks. The comparison between GROUP 0 (low neuroticism level) and GROUP 2 (high neuroticism level) is significant at the .055 level. It is not traditionally significant, but it might be worth paying attention to.

Figure B.3 Annotated SPSS output for a one-way ANOVA with post hoc comparison using the LSD test, The *F* value is significant. The post hoc test indicates one significantly different pair and another that is close and might be worth paying attention to because the theoretical model predicts it.

Tests of Between-Subjects Effects

Dependent Variable: Death-related word fragments

Source	Type III Sum of Squares	df	Mean Square	F	Sig.	Partial Eta Squared
Corrected Model	30.343*	8	3.793	3.099	.002	.068
Intercept	2318.996	1	2318.996	1894.749	.000	.849
Condition	13.257	2	6.628	5.416	.005	.031
NeuroLevel	9.463	2	4.732	3.866	.022	.022
Condition* NeuroLevel	7.730	4	1.933	1.579	.179	.018
Error	413.680	338	1.224			
Total	2820.000	347				
Corrected Total	444.023	346				

> ANOVA summary table for the factorial design. The effect for conditions (joke type) and neuroticism level are both significant, as reflected in *Sig.* values lower than .05. The interaction effect is not significant. We do not normally pay attention to the statistics for *Corrected Model* or *Intercept*.

1. Joke Type

Dependent Variable: Death-related word fragments

Joke Type	Mean	Std. Error	95% Confidence Interval Lower Bound	Upper Bound
0	2.861	.115	2.635	3.087
1	2.364	.102	2.164	2.565
2	2.658	.096	2.469	2.846

2. Neuroticism Level

Dependent Variable: Death-related word fragments

Neuroticism Level	Mean	Std. Error	95% Confidence Interval Lower Bound	Upper Bound
.00	2.401	.103	2.198	2.604
1.00	2.787	.100	2.590	2.984
2.00	2.696	.110	2.479	2.912

> Descriptive statistics for the two independent variables

3. Joke Type * Neuroticism Level

Dependent Variable: Death-related word fragments

Joke Type	Neuroticism Level	Mean	Std. Error	95% Confidence Interval Lower Bound	Upper Bound
0	.00	2.500	.184	2.137	2.863
	1.00	3.324	.190	2.950	3.697
	2.00	2.760	.221	2.325	3.195
1	.00	2.263	.179	1.910	2.616
	1.00	2.317	.173	1.977	2.657
	2.00	2.513	.177	2.164	2.861
2	.00	2.439	.173	2.099	2.779
	1.00	2.720	.156	2.412	3.028
	2.00	2.814	.169	2.482	3.146

> Descriptive statistics for the interaction effects, presenting a breakdown of all individual cell means

Figure B.4   Annotated SPSS summary table and descriptive statistics for 3 × 3 factorial design. The two main effects for the independent variables are statistically significant. The interaction is not significant.

Post Hoc Tests

Joke Type

Multiple Comparisons

> Comparisons of differences by joke type. The asterisks reflect significant effects, with group 0 (death-related jokes) and group 2 (sex-related jokes) equal to each other but differing from the neutral jokes with respect to the number of death-related word fragments they produced.

Death-related word fragments

LSD

(I) Joke Type	(J) Joke Type	Mean Difference (I-J)	Std. Error	Sig.	95% Confidence Interval	
					Lower Bound	Upper Bound
0	1	.50*	.152	.001	.20	.80
	2	.20	.148	.181	-.09	.49
1	0	-.50*	.152	.001	-.80	-.20
	2	-.30*	.140	.033	-.57	-.03
2	0	-.20	.148	.181	-.49	.09
	1	.30*	.140	.033	.03	.57

Based on observed means.
The error term is mean Square(error) - 1.224.
*. The mean difference is significant at the .05 level.

Neuroticism Level

Multiple Comparisons

> Comparison of differences by neuroticism level Significant differences are indicated with asterisks, The comparison between GROUP 0 (low neuroticism level) and GROUP 2 (high neuroticism level) is significant at the .051 level It is not traditionally significant, but it might be worth paying attention to.

Death-related word fragments

LSD

(I) Neuroticism Level	(J) Neuroticism Level	Mean Difference (I-J)	Std. Error	Sig.	95% Confidence Interval	
					Lower Bound	Upper Bound
.00	1.00	-.35*	.143	.014	-.63	-.07
	2.00	-.29	.149	.051	-.58	.00
1.00	.00	.35*	.143	.014	.07	.63
	2.00	.06	.146	.679	-.23	.35
2.00	.00	.29	.149	.051	.00	.58
	1.00	-.06	.146	.679	-.35	.23

Based on observed means.
The error terms is Mean Square(Error) - 1.224.
*. The mean difference is significant at the .05 level.

Figure B.5 Annotated SPSS output for post hoc comparisons using the LSD test for each of the two independent variables. For *Joke Type*, the output indicates that Group 0 (death-related jokes) and Group 1 (sex-related jokes) do not differ in the number of death-related word fragments they generate, but both of these groups lead to a higher incidence of death-related word fragments than does the neutral-joke condition. For neuroticism level, the difference between the low-neuroticism and medium-neuroticism groups is significant at the .051 level; it is worth paying attention to because terror management theory predicts that it should occur.

One-Way ANOVA With Repeated Measures

Step 1	Analyze –> General Linear Model –> Repeated Measures
Step 2	Label the dependent variable that you want in the box *Within-Subject Factor Name*; its default value is *factor1*. (If you do not name the variable, it will simply remain *factor1*.) SPSS will not let you include spaces in the variable name.
Step 3	Type the number of groups on the repeated measures variable in the box labeled *Number of Levels* and click on *Add*.
Step 4	Click on *Define* and move the relevant variables into the box labeled *Within-Subjects Variables*.
Step 5	Click on Options and move your variable into the box labeled *Display Means for.*
Step 6	Check the box labeled *Compare Main Effects*.
Step 7	Check the boxes under *Display* labeled *Descriptive Statistics* and *Estimates of Effect Size*. Click on *Continue*.
Step 8	Select *OK* to tell SPSS to do the computations.

considered statistically significant. But the theory on which the research was based predicted the effect, so it might be reasonable to pay attention to those differences.

If you have a repeated measures design with more than two groups, an ANOVA is appropriate for comparing means of the groups. In the example here, participants rated jokes on a scale of 1 (*not funny*) to 7 (*very funny*). The jokes fell into three categories: jokes that focused on interactions between people, jokes that focused on word play, and jokes that focused on the body. The question was whether participants would rate the jokes as differentially funny depending on the theme of the joke.

As you can see in the SPSS output in Figures B.6 and B.7, the participants rated the jokes differently. Their order of preference for the jokes was interactions, word play, body jokes. The overall effect was statistically significant. Furthermore, a post hoc analysis using the LSD test revealed that each group differed from the other. So participants rated interaction jokes as significantly funnier than verbal jokes, which in turn were seen as funnier than body jokes.

The SPSS output for this analysis can be complicated. I have removed some of the output that SPSS provides from Figures B.6 and B.7 because it isn't particularly relevant for our analysis. What you see in the figures is the important information for understanding the output.

Measure:MEASURE_1

Joketype	Dependent Variable
1	interactionjokes
2	verbaljokes
3	bodyjokes

> Labels of different groups for the independent variable

Descriptive Statistics

	Mean	Std. Deviation	N
interactionjokes	4.3881	1.20358	202
verbaljokes	3.9546	1.25352	202
bodyjokes	3.6361	1.33366	202

> Descriptive statistics for the repeated measures conditions

Mauchly's. Test of Sphericity

Measure:MEASURE_1

Within Subjects Effect	Mauchly's W	Approx. Chi-Square	df	Sig.	Epsilon		
					Greenhouse -Geisser.	Huynh-Feldt	Lower-bound
Joketype	.969	6.378	2	.041	.970	.979	.500

> Test of sphericity. SPSS provides it, but this is not important for a repeated measures analysis involving a single independent variable.

Tests of Within-Subjects Effects

Measure:MEASURE_1

Source		Type III Sum of Squares	df	Mean Square	F	Sig.	Partial Eta Squared
Joketype	Sphericity Assumed	57.558	2	28.779	39.488	.000	.164
	Greenhouse-Geisser	57.558	1.939	29.682	39 488	.000	.164
	Huynh-Feldt	57.558	1.958	29.401	39.488	.000	.164
	Lower-bound	57.558	1.000	57.558	39.488	.000	.164
Error(Joket ype)	Sphericity Assumed	292.981	402	.729			
	Greenhouse-Geisser	292.981	389.766	.752			
	Huynh-Feldt	292.981	393.501	.745			
	Lower-bound	292.981	201.000	1.458			

> ANOVA summary table. For this type of analysis, you can use the output related to *Sphericity Assumed*. The analysis indicates a significant difference in ratings across the three jokes types.

Figure B.6 Annotated SPSS output for a repeated measures analysis involving a single independent variable. The overall analysis indicates a statistically significant effect. Post hoc analysis will reveal which groups differ from one another.

One-Way ANOVA With Repeated Measures With an Additional, Non-repeated Measures Variable

Step 1–8   Follow the steps above for repeated measures variable.

Step 9   Move your non-repeated (i.e., independent measures) independent variable into the box labeled *Between-Subjects Factor(s)*.

Step 10   In the box labeled *Options*, move the non-repeated factor and the interaction term into the box labeled *Display Means for*. (Note: If your non-repeated measures variable has three or more conditions, you can select *Post Hoc* and indicate that you want a post hoc analysis for that variable.)

Step 11   Check the boxes under *Display* labeled *Descriptive Statistics* and *Estimates of Effect Size*. Click on *Continue*.

Step 12   Select *OK* to tell SPSS to do the computations.

Joketype

Estimates

Measure: MEASURE_1

Joketype	Mean	Std. Error	95% Confidence Interval	
			Lower Bound	Upper Bound
1	4.388	.085	4.221	4.555
2	3.955	.088	3.781	4.129
3	3.636	.094	3.451	3.821

> Descriptive statistics for the three repeated measures groups

Pairwise Comparisons

Measure: MEASURE_1

(I) Joketype	(J) Joketype	Mean Difference (I-J)	Std. Error	Sig.*	95% Confidence Interval for Difference*	
					Lower Bound	Upper Bound
1	2	.433*	.085	.000	.266	.601
	3	.752*	.091	.000	.572	.932
2	1	-.433*	.085	.000	-.601	-.266
	3	.318*	.078	.000	.165	.472
3	1	-.752*	.091	.000	-.932	-.572
	2	-.318*	.078	.000	-.472	-.165

Based on estimated marginal means
*. The mean difference is significant at the .05 level.
a. Adjustment for multiple comparisons: Least Significant Difference (equivalent to no adjustments).

> Post-hoc comparisons of groups. Statistically significant differences are indicated by asterisks. The analysis shows that each group differs significantly from every other group. In this case, participants' ratings differed by type of joke.

> Partial Eta Squared indicates the effect size of the experimental manipulation.

Multivariate Tests

	Value	F	Hypothesis df	Error df	Sig.	Partial Eta Squared
Pillai's trace	.253	.33.885*	2.000	200.000	.000	.253
Wilks's lambda	.747	.33.885*	2.000	200.000	.000	.253
Hotelling's trace	.339	.33.885*	2.000	200.000	.000	.253
Roy's largest root	.339	.33.885*	2.000	200.000	.000	.253

Each F tests the multivariate effect of joketype. These tests are based on the linearly independent pairwise comparisons among the estimated marginal means.
a. Exact statistic

Figure B.7   Annotated SPSS output for post hoc analysis involving a repeated measures ANOVA with a single independent variable. The LSD post hoc test indicates that that all three groups differ from one another. There are elements of the SPSS output that do not appear here because they are not relevant for our analysis.

You can also include a non-repeated measures variable in the analysis of a repeated measures variable by following the steps below. You carry out the same steps listed above for repeated measures analyses and continue with the following steps.

This analysis will produce an output that resembles the factorial ANOVA output in some ways. The result of the main effect analysis of the repeated measures variable and the interaction effect will appear in one summary table with the label of *Tests of Within-Subjects Effects*. The non-repeated measures variable with appear in a different summary table labeled *Tests of Between-Subjects Effects*.

If you have conducted a study with multiple repeated measures variables, it would be wise to seek the help of a researcher who is conversant with the complexities of such data analysis. There are issues that you have to consider involving the concept of sphericity, which relates to whether data on repeated measures have equal variances. It is beyond the scope of the presentation here.

Pearson Product-Moment Correlation

Step 1	Analyze –> Correlate –> Repeated Measures
Step 2	Move the variables that you want to correlate into the box labeled *Variables*.
Step 3	Select *OK* to tell SPSS to do the computations.

The correlational analysis in this example involves the association between a participant's score on measures of neuroticism, extraversion, and introversion. The output shows that neuroticism scores correlate negatively with scores on extraversion and on introversion. Thus, low scores on neuroticism are correlated with high scores on extraversion and vice versa. The scores for extraversion and introversion were not significantly correlated. You can see the output in Figure B.8.

Linear Regression

Step 1	Analyze –> Regression –> Linear
Step 2	Move the variable you want to predict (i.e., the criterion variable) into the box labeled *Dependent*.
Step 3	Move the independent (i.e., predictor) variables into the box labeled *Independent(s)*.
Step 4	Select *OK* to tell SPSS to do the computations.

Correlations

> Table of correlations between selected variables. Significant correlations are indicated with asterisks. The *Sig.* value indicates the level of significance.

Correlations

		Neuroticism	Extraversion	Introversion
Neuroticism	Pearson Correlation	1	-.272**	.098
	Sig. (2-tailed)		.000	.069
	N	347	347	347
Extraversion	Pearson Correlation	-.272**	1	-.320**
	Sig. (2-tailed)	.000		.000
	N	347	348	348
Introversion	Pearson Correlation	.098	-.320**	1
	Sig. (2-tailed)	.069	.000	
	N	347	348	348

**.Correlation is significant at the 0.01 level (2-tailed).

> In these examples, the significant correlations are negative, indicating that as neuroticism level increased, extraversion level decreased among participants. Similarly, as extraversion level increased, introversion level decreased.

Figure B.8   Annotated SPSS output indicating correlations between variables. The significant correlations in this example are negative, reflecting the fact that as the value of one variable increased, the value of the other decreased. The correlation between neuroticism and introversion was not statistically significant.

You can conduct linear regression analysis with any number of predictor variables. In this example, we are using self-reports of the degree to which participants (a) produce humor and (b) use humor to cope in order to predict their joke ratings. You should select your predictor variables cautiously because if the predictor variables are themselves correlated, the result of your analysis can be quite confusing.

The output in Figure B.9 indicates that these two predictors together produce a model that is better at predicting joke ratings than simply using the mean as your prediction. If the model were not significant, the mean would be the best overall prediction about a participant's ratings. The model shows that participants' self-reports about their humor production are a significant predictor of joke ratings, but knowing the degree to which they use humor to cope doesn't add to the predictive ability.

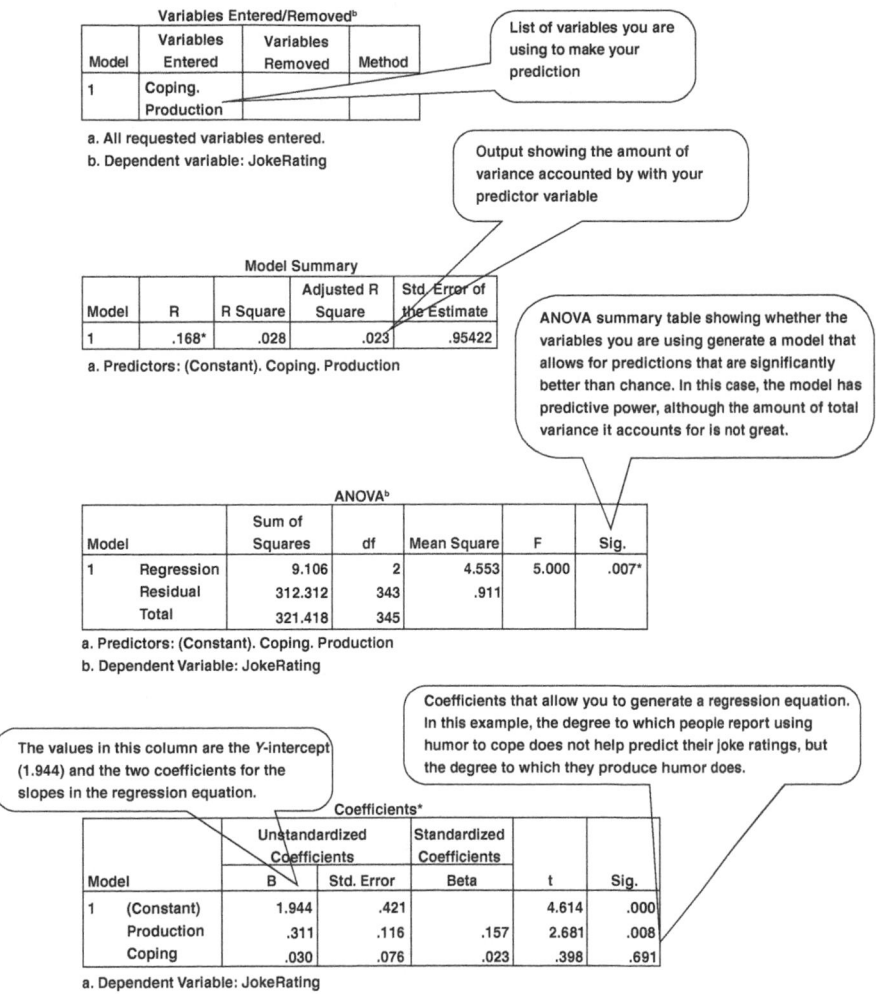

Figure B.9   Annotated SPSS output for linear regression involving two predictor variables. The model provides a small degree of predictability above chance levels.

References

2010 Amendments to the 2002 "Ethical principles of psychologists and code of conduct." (2010). *American Psychologist, 65*, 493. doi:10.1037/a0020168

ACHRE Report. (n.d.). Retrieved July 18, 2012, from http://www.hss.doe.gov/healthsafety/ohre/roadmap/achre/chap7.html

Adachi, P. C., & Willoughby, T. (2011). The effect of video game competition and violence on aggressive behavior: Which characteristic has the greatest influence? *Psychology of Violence, 1*, 259–274. doi:10.1037/a0024908

American Psychological Association. (1953). *Ethical standards of psychologists.* Washington, DC: Author.

American Psychological Association. (2002). Ethical principles of psychologists and code of conduct. (2002). *American Psychologist, 57*, 1060–1073. doi:10.1037/0003-066X.57.12.1060

American Psychological Association (2010). *Publication manual of the American Psychological Association* (6th ed.). Washington, DC: Author.

Anderson, C. A., & Bushman, B. J. (2002). Media violence and the American public revisited. *American Psychologist, 57*, 448–450. doi:10.1037/0003-066X.57.6-7.448

Bargh, J. A., Chen, M., & Burrows, L. (1996). Automaticity of social behavior: Direct effects of trait construct and stereotype activation on action. *Journal of Personality and Social Psychology, 71*(2), 230–244. doi:10.1037/0022-3514.71.2.230

Bartlett, T. (2012, April 17). Is psychology about to come undone? *Chronicle of Higher Education.* Retrieved from http://chronicle.com/blogs/percolator/is-psychology-about-to-come-undone/29045

Beins, B. C., Doychak, K., Ferrante, P., Herschman, C., & Sherry, S. (2012, October). Jokes and terror management theory: Humor may not help manage terror. Poster presentation at the annual convention of the New England Psychological Association, Worcester, MA.

Beins, B. C., & O'Toole, S. M. (2010). Searching for the sense of humor: Stereotypes of ourselves and others. *Europe's Journal of Psychology, 6*, 3/2010, 267–287. Available at http://www.ejop.org/archives/2010/08/index.html

Beins, B. C. (2012). *APA style simplified: Writing in psychology, education, nursing, and sociology.* Malden, MA: Wiley-Blackwell.

Belmont Report. (1979). Retrieved July 18, 2012, from http://www.hhs.gov/ohrp/humansubjects/guidance/belmont.html

Bem, D. J. (2011). Feeling the future: Experimental evidence for anomalous retroactive influences on cognition and affect. *Journal of Personality and Social Psychology, 100*, 407–425. doi:10.1037/a0021524

Benfante, L., & Beins, B. C. (2007, October). *Self-reflection and sense of humor: The Big Five personality characteristics and humor.* Poster session at the annual convention of the New England Psychological Association, Danbury, CT.

Berkowitz, L. (1970). Aggressive humor as a stimulus to aggressive responses. *Journal of Personality and Social Psychology, 16*, 710–717. doi:10.1037/h0030077

Berlyne, D. (1971). *Aesthetics and Psychology.* New York, NY: Appleton-Century.

Blaskovich, J., & Tomaka, J. (Eds.). (1991), *Measures of self-esteem* (Vol. 1). New York, NY: Academic Press.

Bröder, A. (1998). Deception can be acceptable. *American Psychologist, 53*, 805–806. doi:10.1037/h0092168

Brummert Lennings, H. I., & Warburton, W. A. (2011). The effect of auditory versus visual violent media exposure on aggressive behaviour: The role of song lyrics, video clips and musical tone. *Journal of Experimental Social Psychology, 47*, 794–799. doi:10.1016/j.jesp.2011.02.006

Bryson, B. (2007). *Shakespeare: The world as stage.* New York, NY: HarperCollins.

Buhrmester, M., Kwang, T., & Gosling, S. D. (2011). Amazon's Mechanical Turk: A new source of inexpensive, yet high-quality, data? *Perspectives on Psychological Science, 6*, 3–5. doi:10.1177/1745691610393980

Bushman, B. J., & Anderson, C. A. (2001). Media violence and the American public: Scientific facts versus media misinformation. *American Psychologist, 56*, 477–489. doi:10.1037/0003-066X.56.6-7.477

Casasanto, D. (2009). Embodiment of abstract concepts: Good and bad in right- and left-handers. *Journal of Experimental Psychology: General, 138*, 351–367. doi:10.1037/a0015854

Code of Federal Regulations. (2010). Retrieved July 18, 2012, from http://www.hhs.gov/ohrp/humansubjects/guidance/45cfr46.html

Cohen, J. (1988). *Statistical power analysis for the behavioral sciences.* Hillsdale, NJ: Erlbaum.

Cooper, P. J., Taylor, M. J., Cooper, Z., & Fairburn, C. G. (1987). The development and validation of the Body Shape Questionnaire. *International Journal of Eating Disorders, 6*, 485–494. doi:10.1002/1098-108X(198707)6:4<485::AID-EAT2260060405>3.0.CO;2

Coren, S., & Halpern, D. F. (1991). Left-handedness: A marker for decreased survival fitness. *Psychological Bulletin, 109*, 90–106. doi:10.1037/0033-2909.109.1.90

Darley, J. M., & Latané, B. (1968). Bystander intervention in emergencies: Diffusion of responsibility. *Journal of Personality and Social Psychology, 8*, 377–383. doi:10.1037/h0025589

Dietz, A. P., Albowicz, C., & Beins, B. C. (2011, October). *Neuroticism and sex-related jokes: Predictions from terror management theory.* Poster presentation at the annual convention of the New England Psychological Association, Fairfield, CT.

Doychak, K., Herschman, C., Ferrante, P., & Beins, B. C. (2012, March). *Sense of humor: Are we all above average?* Poster session at the annual convention of the Eastern Psychological Association, Pittsburgh, PA.

Elliot, A. J., & Thrash, T. M. (2004). The intergenerational transmission of fear of failure. *Personality and Social Psychology Bulletin, 30,* 957–971. doi:10.1177/0146167203262024

Epstude, K., & Förster, J. (2011). Seeing love, or seeing lust: How people interpret ambiguous romantic situations. *Journal of Experimental Social Psychology, 47,* 1017–1020. doi:10.1016/j.jesp.2011.03.019

Ferguson, C. J. (2002). Media violence: Miscast causality. *American Psychologist, 57,* 446–447. doi:10.1037/0003-066X.57.6-7.446b

Ferring, D., & Filipp, S. (1996). Messung des Selbstwertgefühls: Befunde zu Reliabilität, Validität und Stabilität der Rosenberg-Skala. *Diagnostica, 42,* 284–292.

Galloway, G., & Chirico, D. (2008). Personality and humor appreciation: Evidence of an association between trait neuroticism and preferences for structural features of humor. *Humor: International Journal of Humor Research, 21,* 129–142. doi:10.1515/HUMOR.2008.006

Glick, P., & Fiske, S. T. (1996). The Ambivalent Sexism Inventory: Differentiating hostile and benevolent sexism. *Journal of Personality and Social Psychology, 70,* 491–512. doi:10.1037/0022-3514.70.3.491

Glick, P., & Fiske, S. T. (1999). The Ambivalence Toward Men Inventory: Differentiating hostile and benevolent beliefs about men. *Psychology of Women Quarterly, 23,* 519–536. doi:10.1111/j.1471-6402.1999.tb00379.x

Goldenberg, J. L., Pyszczynski, T., Greenberg, J., Solomon, S., Kluck, B., & Cornwell, R. (2001). I am not an animal: Mortality salience, disgust, and the denial of human creatureliness. *Journal of Experimental Psychology: General, 130,* 427–435. doi:10.1037/0096-3445.130.3.427

Goldenberg, J. L., Pyszczynski, T., McCoy, S. K., Greenberg, J., & Solomon, S. (1999). Death, sex, love, and neuroticism: Why is sex such a problem? *Journal of Personality and Social Psychology, 77,* 1173–1187.

Good, C., Rattan, A., & Dweck, C. S. (2012). Why do women opt out? Sense of belonging and women's representation in mathematics. *Journal of Personality and Social Psychology, 102,* 700–717. doi:10.1037/a0026659

Gosling, S. D., Vazire, S., Srivastava, S., & John, O. P. (2004). Should we trust web-based studies? A comparative analysis of six preconceptions about internet questionnaires. *American Psychologist, 59,* 93–104. doi:10.1037/0003-066X.59.2.93

Greenwald, A. G., & Banaji, M. R. (1995). Implicit social cognition: Attitudes, self-esteem, and stereotypes. *Psychological Review, 102,* 4-27. doi:10.1037/0033-295X .102.1.4

Grumm, M., Nestler, S., & von Collani, G. (2009). Changing explicit and implicit attitudes: The case of self-esteem. *Journal of Experimental Social Psychology, 45,* 327–335. doi:10.1016/j.jesp.2008.10.006

Haidt, J., McCauley, C., & Rozin, P. (1994). Individual differences in sensitivity to disgust: A scale sampling seven domains of disgust elicitors. *Personality and Individual Differences, 16,* 701–713. doi:10.1016/0191-8869(94)90212-7

Hehl, F., & Ruch, W. (1985). The location of sense of humor within comprehensive personality spaces: An exploratory study. *Personality and Individual Differences, 6,* 703–715. doi:10.1016/0191-8869(85)90081-9

Helzer, E. G., & Dunning, D. (2012). Why and when peer prediction is superior to self-prediction: The weight given to future aspiration versus past achievement. *Journal of Personality and Social Psychology, 103,* 38–53. doi:10.1037/a0028124

Hertwig, R., & Ortmann, A. (2008). Deception in social psychological experiments: Two misconceptions and a research agenda. *Social Psychology Quarterly, 71*(3), 222–227. doi:10.1177/019027250807100304

Hilts, P. J., & Stolberg, S. G. (1999, May 13). Ethical lapses at Duke halt dozens of human experiments. *New York Times.* Retrieved July 18, 2012, from www.nytimes.com/1999/05/13/us/ethics-lapses-at-duke-halt-dozens-of-human-experiments.html

Hoffmeister, K., Teige-Mocigemba, S., Blechert, J., Klauer, K., & Tuschen-Caffier, B. (2010). Is implicit self-esteem linked to shape and weight concerns in restrained and unrestrained eaters? *Journal of Behavior Therapy and Experimental Psychiatry, 41,* 31–38. doi:10.1016/j.jbtep.2009.08.009

Horner, M. S. (1972). Toward an understanding of achievement-related conflicts in women. *Journal of Social Issues, 28,* 157–175.

Howell, D. C. (2007). *Statistical methods for psychology* (6th ed.). Belmont, CA: Thomson Wadsworth.

Instructions in regard to preparation of manuscript. (1929). *The Psychological Bulletin, 26,* 57–63. doi:10.1037/h0071487

Ioannidis, J. P. A. (2005). Why most published research findings are false. *PLoS Med 2*(8): e124. doi:10.1371/journal.pmed.0020124

Ippolito, A., & Beins, B. C. (2011, March). *Personality and humor: How accurate are our reflections of ourselves?* Presented at the annual convention of the Eastern Psychological Association, Cambridge, MA.

Kasof, J. (1993). Sex bias in the naming of stimulus persons. *Psychological Bulletin, 113,* 140–163. doi:10.1037/0033-2909.113.1.140

Kitayama, S., & Karasawa, M. (1997). Implicit self-esteem in Japan: Name letters and birthday numbers. *Personality and Social Psychology Bulletin, 23,* 736–742. doi:10.1177/0146167297237006

Koehler, D. J., & Poon, C. S. K. (2006). Self-predictions overweight the strength of current intentions. *Journal of Experimental Social Psychology, 42,* 517–524. doi:10.1016/j.jesp.2005.08.003

Korn, J. H. (1998). The reality of deception. *American Psychologist, 53*(7), doi:10.1037/0003-066X.53.7.805.b

Landau, M. J., Goldenberg, J. L., Greenberg, J., Gillath, O., Solomon, S., Cox, C. . . . Pyszczynski, T. (2006). The siren's call: Terror management and the threat of men's sexual attraction to women. *Journal of Personality and Social Psychology, 90*, 129–146. doi:10.1037/0022-3514.90.1.129

Larrick, R. P., Timmerman, T. A., Carton, A. M., & Abrevaya, J. (2011). Temper, temperature, and temptation: Heat-related retaliation in baseball. *Psychological Science, 22*, 423–428. doi:10.1177/0956797611399292

LeBel, E. P., & Gawronski, B. (2009). How to find what's in a name: Scrutinizing the optimality of five scoring algorithms for the name-letter task. *European Journal of Personality, 23*, 85–106. doi:10.1002/per.705

Lieberman, J. D., Solomon, S., Greenberg, J., & McGregor, H. A. (1999). A hot new way to measure aggression: Hot sauce allocation. *Aggressive Behavior, 25*, 331–348. doi:10.1002/(SICI)1098-2337(1999)25:5<331::AID-AB2>3.0.CO;2-1

Manning, R., Levine, M., & Collins, A. (2007). The Kitty Genovese murder and the social psychology of helping: The parable of the 38 witnesses. *American Psychologist, 62*, 555–562. doi:10.1037/0003-066X.62.6.555

Marsh, J. E., Beaman, C., Hughes, R. W., & Jones, D. M. (2012). Inhibitory control in memory: Evidence for negative priming in free recall. *Journal of Experimental Psychology: Learning, Memory, and Cognition.* doi:10.1037/a0027849

Martin, R. A., & Lefcourt, H. M. (1984). Situational Humor Response Questionnaire: Quantitative measure of sense of humor. *Journal of Personality and Social Psychology, 47*, 145–155. doi:10.1037/0022-3514.47.1.145

Meijboom, A., Jansen, A., Kampman, M., & Schouten, E. (1999). An experimental test of the relationship between self-esteem and concern about body shape and weight in restrained eaters. *International Journal of Eating Disorders, 25*, 327–334. doi:10.1002/(SICI)1098-108X(199904)25:3<327::AID-EAT11>3.0.CO;2-5

Meijer, A., & van den Wittenboer, G. H. (2004). The joint contribution of sleep, intelligence and motivation to school performance. *Personality and Individual Differences, 37*, 95–106. doi:10.1016/j.paid.2003.08.002

Metzler, J. N., & Conroy, D. E. (2004). Structural validity of the Fear of Success Scale. *Measurement in Physical Education and Exercise Science, 8*, 89–108. doi:10.1207/s15327841mpee0802_4

Milgram, S. (1974). *Obedience to authority: An experimental view.* New York, NY: Harper & Row.

Mitchell, G. (2012). Revisiting truth or triviality: The external validity of research in the psychological laboratory. *Pesrpectives on Psychological Science, 7*, 109–117. doi:10.1177/1745691611432343

Nuttin, J. M. (1985). Narcissism beyond Gestalt and awareness: The name letter effect. *European Journal of Social Psychology, 15*, 353–361. doi:10.1002/ejsp.2420150309

Nuttin, J. M. (1987). Affective consequences of mere ownership: The name letter effect in twelve European languages. *European Journal of Social Psychology, 17*, 381–402. doi:10.1002/ejsp.2420170402

Olatunji, B. O., Williams, N. L., Tolin, D. F., Abramowitz, J. S., Sawchuk, C. N., Lohr, J. M., & Elwood, L. S. (2007). The Disgust Scale: Item analysis, factor structure, and suggestions for refinement. *Psychological Assessment, 19,* 281–297. doi:10.1037/1040-3590.19.3.281

On the newsstand. (2009, January). *Observer, 22*(1), 8.

Ortmann, A., & Hertwig, R. (1997). Is deception acceptable? *American Psychologist, 52*(7), 746–747. doi:10.1037/0003-066X.52.7.746

Peetz, J., & Buehler, R. (2009). Is there a budget fallacy? The role of savings goals in the prediction of personal spending. *Personality and Social Psychology Bulletin, 35,* 1579 –1591. doi:10.1177/0146167209345160

Rauscher, F. H., & Shaw, G. L. (1998). Key components of the Mozart effect. *Perceptual and Motor Skills, 86*(3, Pt. 1), 835–841. doi:10.2466/pms.1998.86.3.835

Rauscher, F. H., Shaw, G. L., & Ky, K. N. (1993). Music and spatial-task performance. *Nature, 365,* 611. doi:10.1038/365611a0

Reifman, A. S., Larrick, R. P., & Fein, S. (1991). Temper and temperature on the diamond: The heat-aggression relationship in major league baseball. *Personality and Social Psychology Bulletin, 17,* 580–585. doi:10.1177/0146167291175013

Riketta, M., & Dauenheimer, D. (2003). Manipulating self-esteem with subliminally presented words. *European Journal of Social Psychology, 33,* 679–699. doi:10.1002/ejsp.179

Ritchie, S. J., Wiseman, R., & French, C. C. (2012). Failing the future: Three unsuccessful attempts to replicate Bem's "retroactive facilitation of recall" effect. *PLoS ONE 7*(3): e33423. doi:10.1371/journal.pone.0033423

Robinson, J. P., Shaver, P. R., & Wrightsman, L. S. (Eds.). (1991). *Measures of personality and social psychological attitudes.* San Diego, CA: Academic Press.

Rosenberg, M. (1965). *Society and adolescent self-image.* Princeton, NJ: Princeton University Press.

Rosenberg, M. (1979). *Conceiving the self.* New York, NY: Basic Books.

Rothman, D. J. (1994, January 9). Government guinea pigs. *New York Times,* Section 4, p. 23.

Schwartz, B. M., Landrum, R. E., & Gurung, R. A. R. (2012). *An easy guide to APA style.* Los Angeles, CA: Sage.

Scientists highlight link between stress and appetite. (2011, August 13). Retrieved August 26, 2011, from http://www.sciencedaily.com/releases/2011/08/110812213034.htm

Seegmiller, J. K., Watson, J. M., & Strayer, D. L. (2011). Individual differences in susceptibility to inattentional blindness. *Journal of Experimental Psychology: Learning, Memory, and Cognition, 37,* 785–791. doi:10.1037/a0022474

Sinclair, S. J., Blais, M. A., Gansler, D. A., Sandberg, E., Bistis, K., & LoCicero, A. (2010). Psychometric properties of the Rosenberg Self-Esteem Scale: Overall and across demographic groups living within the United States. *Evaluation & the Health Professions, 33,* 56–80. doi:10.1177/0163278709356187

Smith, P. C. (2007). Assessing students' research ideas. In D. S. Dunn, R. A. Smith, & B. C. Beins (Eds.), *Best practices for teaching statistics and research methods in the behavioral sciences* (pp. 59–70). Mahwah, NJ: Lawrence Erlbaum Associates.

Song, H., & Schwarz, N. (2008). If it's hard to read, it's hard to do: Processing fluency affects effort prediction and motivation. *Psychological Science, 19*, 986–988. doi:10.1111/j.1467-9280.2008.02189.x

Song, H., & Schwarz, N. (2009). If it's difficult to pronounce, it must be risky: Fluency, familiarity, and risk perception. *Psychological Science, 20*, 135–138. doi:10.1111/j.1467-9280.2009.02267.x

Steele, K. M., Bass, K. E., & Crook, M. D. (1999). The mystery of the Mozart effect: Failure to replicate. *Psychological Science, 10*, 366–369. doi:10.1111/1467-9280.00169

Svaldi, J. J., Zimmermann, S. S., & Naumann, E. E. (2012). The impact of an implicit manipulation of self-esteem on body dissatisfaction. *Journal of Behavior Therapy and Experimental Psychiatry, 43*, 581–586. doi:10.1016/j.jbtep.2011.08.003

Thomas, R. C., & Hasher, L. (2012). Reflections of distraction in memory: Transfer of previous distraction improves recall in younger and older adults. *Journal of Experimental Psychology: Learning, Memory, and Cognition, 38*, 30–39. doi:10.1037/a0024882

Thorson, J. A., & Powell, F. C. (1993a). Development and validation of a multidimensional sense of humor scale. *Journal of Clinical Psychology, 49*, 13–23. doi:10.1002/1097-4679(199301)49:1<13::AID-JCLP2270490103>3.0.CO;2

Thorson, J. A., & Powell, F. C. (1993b). Sense of humor and dimensions of personality. *Journal of Clinical Psychology, 49*, 799–809. doi:10.1002/1097-4679(199311)49:6<799::AID-JCLP2270490607>3.0.CO;2-P

Tollefson, D. L., & Cattell, R. B. (1963). *Handbook for the IPAT Humor Test of Personality*. Champaign, IL: Institute for Personality and Ability Testing.

Uysal, A., & Knee, C. (2012). Low trait self-control predicts self-handicapping. *Journal of Personality, 80*, 59–79. doi:10.1111/j.1467-6494.2011.00715.x

Von Hentig, H. (1947). Redhead and outlaw: A study in criminal anthropology. *Journal of Criminal Law & Criminology, 38*, 1–6.

Webster, G. D., Urland, G. R., & Correll, J. (2012). Can uniform color color aggression? Quasi-experimental evidence from professional ice hockey. *Social Psychological and Personality Science, 3*, 274–281.doi: 10.1177/1948550611418535

Williams, M., & Woodman, G. F. (2012). Directed forgetting and directed remembering in visual working memory. *Journal of Experimental Psychology: Learning, Memory, and Cognition, 38*, 1206–1220. doi:10.1037/a0027389

Williamson, D. A., Muller, S. L., Reas, D. L., & Thaw, J. M. (1999). Cognitive bias in eating disorders: Implications for theory and treatment. *Behavior Modification, 23*, 556–577. doi:10.1177/0145445599234003

Wimer, D. J., & Beins, B. C. (2008). Expectation and perceived humor. *Humor: International Journal of Humor Studies, 21*, 347–363.

Witt, J. K., & Brockmole, J. R. (2012). Action alters object identification: Wielding a gun increases the bias to see guns. *Journal of Experimental Psychology:*

Human Perception and Performance. Advance online publication. doi:10.1037/a0027881

Zimbardo, P. G. (1973). On the ethics of intervention in human psychological research: With special reference to the Stanford prison experiment. *Cognition, 2,* 243–256. doi:10.1016/0010-0277(72)90014-5

Zuckerman, M., & Allison, S. N. (1976). An objective measure of fear of success: Construction and validation. *Journal of Personality Assessment, 40,* 422–430. doi:10.1207/s15327752jpa4004_12a

Index

About the Author ❖

Bernard C. (Barney) Beins is professor of psychology at Ithaca College. He is a past recipient of the Charles L. Brewer Distinguished Teaching Award from the American Psychological Foundation. He is a fellow of APA Divisions 2 (Teaching of Psychology), 3 (Experimental Psychology), and 52 (International Psychology), the Association for Psychological Science, and the Eastern Psychological Association.

He has served as president and as secretary of the Society for the Teaching of Psychology. In addition, he was director of Precollege and Undergraduate Education at American Psychological Association (APA) and has been a member of APA's Board of Educational Affairs and Council of Representatives. In addition, he is a member of the test development committee for the Psychology test of the Graduate Record Exam, and he served as chair of the test development committee for the Advanced Placement test in Psychology.

Much of his professional work involves the scholarship of teaching and learning, particularly writing, critical thinking, and research methods. In addition, he and his students conduct research on humor.

He authored *Research Methods: A Tool for Life* and *APA Style Simplified*. He has coauthored two editions of *Effective Writing in Psychology* with his daughter Agatha Beins and *Research Methods and Statistics* with Maureen McCarthy. He has also authored or coedited another two dozen book-length products and about 150 journal articles, book chapters, encyclopedia entries, and reviews. He has given over 200 presentations; his students have made over 100.

His work has included participation in APA's National Conference on Undergraduate Psychology, the St. Mary's Conference, and the Psychology Partnerships Project. He founded the Northeastern Conference for Teachers of Psychology, which continues in conjunction with the New England Psychological Association convention. He was e-books editor for the

Society for the Teaching of Psychology and editor of the Computers in Psychology section of *Teaching of Psychology*. He currently edits the Teaching of History section of the journal *History of Psychology*.

He earned his bachelor's degree from Miami University in Oxford, Ohio, and his doctorate from City University of New York.

⑨SAGE research**methods**

The essential online tool for researchers from the world's leading methods publisher

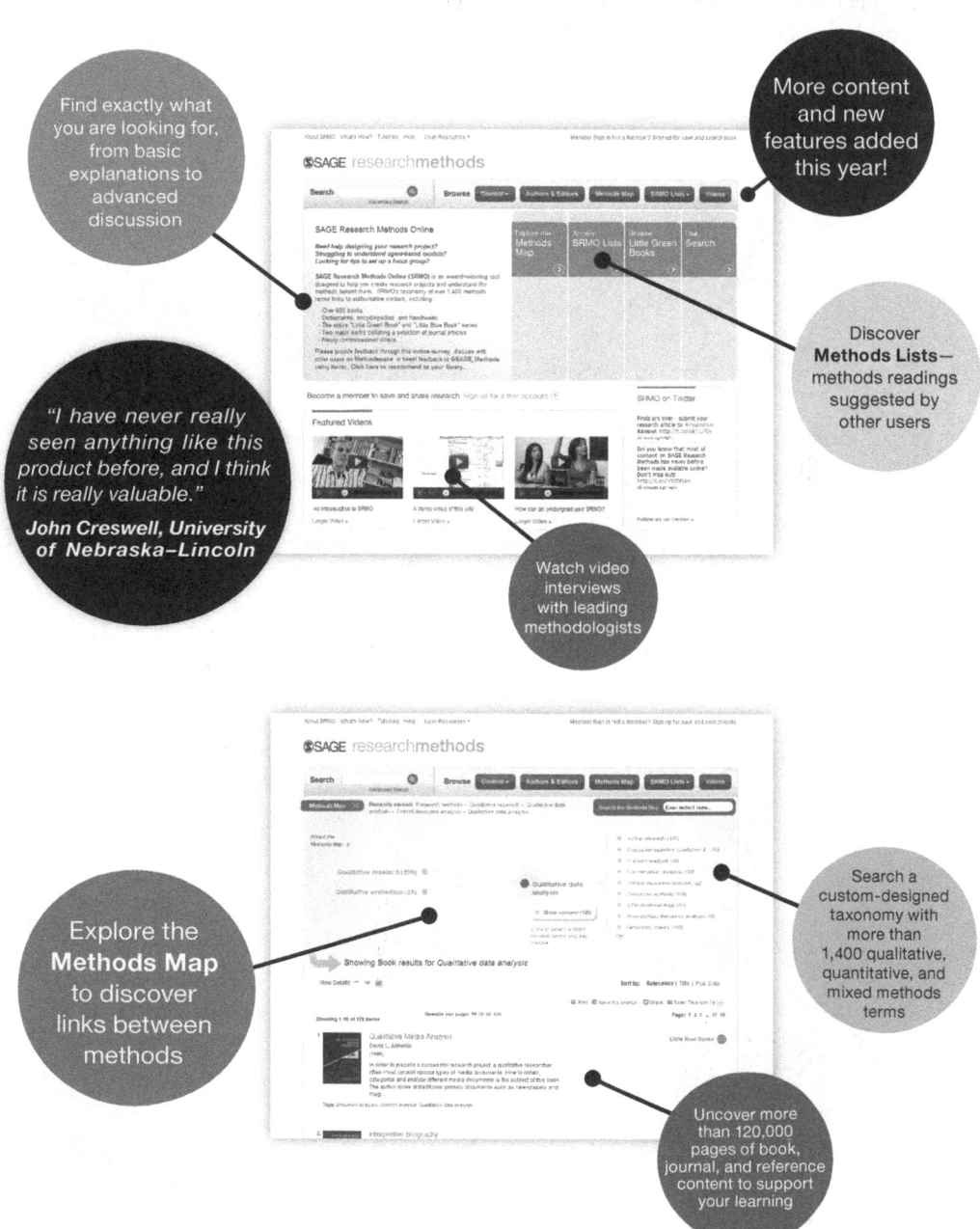

Find exactly what you are looking for, from basic explanations to advanced discussion

More content and new features added this year!

Discover **Methods Lists**— methods readings suggested by other users

"I have never really seen anything like this product before, and I think it is really valuable."
John Creswell, University of Nebraska–Lincoln

Watch video interviews with leading methodologists

Explore the **Methods Map** to discover links between methods

Search a custom-designed taxonomy with more than 1,400 qualitative, quantitative, and mixed methods terms

Uncover more than 120,000 pages of book, journal, and reference content to support your learning

Find out more at
www.sageresearchmethods.com